Biography

of a

Wildman

Grant Shorfield

authorHOUSE®

AuthorHouse™
1663 Liberty Drive
Bloomington, IN 47403
www.authorhouse.com
Phone: 1-800-839-8640

Published by AuthorHouse   11/01/2012

ISBN: 978-1-4772-1431-2 (sc)
ISBN: 978-1-4772-1432-9 (e)

Grant began writing in the spring of 1975 when he finally took charge of his life and dumped his long standing girlfriend; he hadn't realised it, but the relationship had died about three years earlier when she whacked him across the shins with a poker. Grant eventually recovered, put two and two together, and limped away to start a new life. Things could only get better.

He discovered loneliness. Somehow, he had to fill his days. He spent a great deal of time trying to learn to play the piano; there was partial success as he is now able to play a very poor rendition of 'The Entertainer'. Realising that the piano was not his passport to success he decided to have a go at writing. He hasn't stopped.

Biography of a Wildman is volume two and was written first as the memories were still very fresh and seemed to demand immediate recording. Volume one, the early years, came next and then volume three. Volumes one to three were typed up rather painfully on a dilapidated portable typewriter. In those days, portable meant it wasn't bolted to the floor. Being wholly mechanical, the action of typing required considerable force on the fingers—writing hurt! Modern computers make the process so easy—the brain numbing process of editing and redrafting is made so much easier. Volumes four and five were somewhat delayed by the intervention of children—they are so time consuming and messy! Volume six is in the pipeline.

Why on earth has Grant gone to so much trouble and effort, to record events that happened to an individual with no fame or public recognition? The answer is simple—Grant has collided with the unusual and peculiar all his life. He has often found himself to be a running mate with weird individuals and absurd events. Have you ever applied for a job and been set a task that you couldn't do? Have you walked out after ten minutes realising you were out of your depth? Did you turn down the invitation for an interview at least three times before reluctantly accepting? Did you attend the interview though everything told you it was a waste of time? Grant did. Oh, and he got the job—one that he really enjoyed.

Grant was the first member of his family to continue with full time education; he has been a teacher of mathematics and other related subjects since 1972. He has taught students aged from five through to pensioners—but not all at the same time or in the same class of course. He has lived in the London area and the southeast corner of England all his life. He met his wife in 1978; they are married and have three children and three grandchildren—and the prospect of more. Grant has numerous interests that include making wine (which is truly disgusting—his birch sap wine was particularly lethal), playing the Spanish guitar moderately well, a writer of songs that make Leonard Cohen sound positively happy and a surprisingly wide range of practical skills that have saved a fortune on plumbing, electrics and general building tasks. Grant has surprisingly poor linguistic skills; he has been learning Spanish since 1988 and he still sounds 'muy horrible'. On the other hand, his daughter says that, were she shipwrecked, she'd want her Dad to be along as he'd be able to build a boat and a radio from coconut shells.

By publishing this book, Grant has joined a family of writers; his eldest brother has written his autobiography and his younger sister has written science fiction and fantasy novels—not bad for a family from very humble working class origins.

FROM THE AUTHOR

I must thank my daughter for proof reading and making critical suggestions. The images were suggested by her; so that's all her fault. I have to apologise to her husband who had to put up with her constant chuckling as she read each exploit unfolding on the manuscript.

I must say thanks to my wife for bearing with me and hearing these stories over and over again—for her it was a case of 'a story told too often's told too well'. Many friends and acquaintances have heard the tales of Mick and me but my wife has had to put up with it for decades—thank you.

I have a long overdue thank you for the friends who read the original handwritten draft and were so encouraging four decades ago. I told you I'd get it finished one day.

Finally, I would like to add a thank you to my mother-in-law for typing up the first electronic version. She is a skilled touch-typist but she kept losing her place; she was getting too involved with the 'stories' and found herself repeatedly having to stop. She would ring me up and ask me, 'Grant, did you really do those things?'

'What me? Of course not!' I fibbed.

CHAPTER 1

A short history lesson

It was a sunny day and I had been sent out by my biology teacher, Mrs. Thompson, to look at the flowers growing on the school field. Doesn't that sound rather strange! There was logic to it. I was studying A-level biology—in fact, I was the first student at the school in living memory to have taken the subject. I had done well at the 'O Level' stage in science and so my choice of A-level biology fitted my plans. Mrs. Thompson thought me ill-advised and told me I really didn't have a hope in hell of passing it. She told me to stick to mathematics, my stronger subject—at least I had some chance of passing that. Huh! I certainly proved her wrong because I did pass. OK, I got the lowest pass grade but I'd done the course in half the time with no teaching. I did well and was delighted to have proved her wrong.

Despite the negativity coming from Mrs. Thompson, I enjoyed studying biology a great deal. My teacher, well, she was really hard-nosed but she thought she was 'ok'—she wasn't. She thought her students loved her—they didn't. She was too unpredictable; one moment she was easy and relaxed, the next moment she was an authoritarian. I tend to get on with most people but she was a member of the small group that I am suspicious of. There aren't many out there but I remember them. It takes a lot to get me to move ordinary people into my exclusion zone but a few, just a few, get set apart immediately. Mrs. Thompson was especially confusing because each year she would take a party of older students away to a residential centre. There was a programme of work to go with the trip but, on the whole, most of the time was given over to walking and having a good time. Mrs. Thompson relaxed considerably and even managed to smuggle some of the older students into a local pub for a drink. We enjoyed the relaxed atmosphere and grew to like her but, as soon as we were back in school, she became a dragon again. Anyway, that's rather getting off the point and I'm only on my second paragraph. This could be a difficult journey we're set on.

So, having been told to study the plant life I made my way outside and went off to do what was expected of me; after a short while the school grounds man came across and spoke to me. He seemed to know a great deal about botany and we chatted for perhaps an hour before I had to go back to the lesson that I had left. These 'field' studies were infrequent but each time I went out, the grounds man would sense my presence and then come over and we would chat. Each time he gave me more useful information and eventually we were on a first name basis. I learnt then that his name was Mick. After a few of these contacts with Mick I told Mrs. Thompson that he was helping me with my studies and she stiffened noticeably—she told me to be on my guard against him and to watch myself carefully. I took no notice since I thought she was just going on for the sake of it—she usually did. Anyway what could she possibly know that I, at sixteen, didn't know already?

I soon realised that Mick was a peculiar person but in the early days of our friendship I couldn't quite work out why. I was hardly worldly wise. My dealings with him were almost totally confined to the school field—I didn't witness any of his 'interesting' activities, at first hand, for some time. My school friends told me curious stories about him that I disbelieved, and yet Mick himself later admitted they were essentially true. He had a large hut in which was stored the gardening equipment, rollers, shovels and other 'implements of destruction' and such like. Unknown to the teachers, Mick turned this hut into an unofficial cinema and showed films to the kids. His films were all cheap and rather tacky sex films. They were silent cine films so they hardly lasted any time at all; only a couple of minutes. One I remember was a black and white film about a Swedish woman washing her breasts. The kids all used to love this and they'd be jerking off. If he was allowed, Mick would do it for them, as the flickering image of the blonde beauty carried out her bathing antics. Between films, Mick would serve refreshments to the kids; orange squash served up in dirty, cracked cups. He had no idea of cleanliness—he simply filled the empty cups as and when he wished to. Perhaps now and then he would shake out the dried lumps but this was discretionary.

The water for the drinks came from a tank in the roof of the hut. This tank was fed by rainwater that fell onto the sloping roof, into the gutters and then entered via a rusty pipe. The kids had no idea of this situation and being kids of the time probably wouldn't have cared anyway (I can't imagine our 'modern' designer label generation acting quite so laid back about it). Mick admitted that one day he had to clean out the tank because no water would come out of it. He climbed up into the loft space and took the ill-fitting lid off. Inside he found the rotting remains of a pigeon. The corpse was so rotten that it had almost dissolved—bits of flesh had blocked up the pipe as they had been swept along by the water flow. Mick scooped out as much of the pigeon as he could and then it was business as normal. He told me he was rather amused by it. The orange cordial obviously masked the taste extremely well.

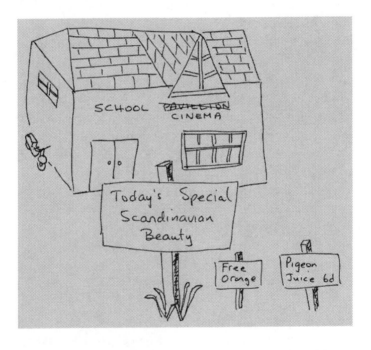

None of the boys ever complained of stomach problems, so there was never any comeback. Mick also served tea and coffee to those with more adult tastes. They used filthy cups and mugs and the same supply of disgusting water.

Mick was in his early thirties and a superficial glance at him would have seen a perfectly normal man. He had a healthy head of black wavy hair that usually needed a trim; he was clean shaven and wore casual clothing most of the time. At work he tended to wear overalls or jeans and a rather shabby work jacket. He was of average height and fairly slim. He didn't smoke as a habit but he scrounged a smoke when the feeling took him.

As our friendship grew so Mick became very keen to share his history with me and he told me a great deal about himself and his family. He told me about how he grew up in the East End of London before, during and after the Second World War. His father had been a religious fanatic who had gone to Speaker's Corner, in Hyde Park, Central London, every Sunday. He went there to preach. He would wear a huge top hat and long coat and, standing on a pair of stepladders, he'd rant and rave about God, sinners and his religious beliefs in general. Sometimes, Mick, along with his brothers and sisters, had to go up and watch and attend as supporters. His father was loud and outspoken and gathered a large crowd who reacted to his words with laughter, shouting and abuse. Mick's father always seemed to rise to the occasion and was fully able to use threats of the 'wrath of God' in his retorts to the heckling. Mick loathed his father but some of the ideas rubbed off onto him and Mick incorporated some of the extreme ideas from his father in his own theological and zany approach—the ideas were taken on in his own modified and often rather lunatic version. I had the luck of seeing a photograph of the father—he stood upon his step-ladder looking both demented and starving—Mick agreed that he was both.

Mick's family were so poor; it was a surprise that the stepladders were not pawned off, but I suppose, they were instruments in the delivery of the words of God and so they couldn't be dispensed with.

Mick's family had lived in a very deprived neighbourhood and the children in his family, like those living around them, were usually dressed in cast-offs and ill-fitting clothes that were rudely patched and hardly held together. The name of the game was to survive and that was all they could do. Life was hard and the future prospects seemed just to be an endless grind of more of the same. As a boy, Mick had witnessed firsthand the destruction of the East End during the Blitz. Mick didn't speak negatively about it; he told his stories of collecting shell fragments from the street and playing in bombed out houses as though it was just another playground. I asked him about the bombed out houses and whether or not people had looted them. Mick told me about how he and his friends used to visit the fresh sites to see if there was any jewellery or other valuables. There weren't many because people didn't have very much. Most of the time, Mick and his friends simply went into the bombed out sites and smashed things—just for the hell of it. Even if they did find things they couldn't take them home because Mick's dad would have asked them where they had got them from—then he would have beaten them senseless.

At one point the family was so destitute that they had a terrible problem with clothing and shoes. Replacing clothing was the easier of the two problems as garments could be handed down from older to younger sibling. Shoes were a much bigger problem because they actually wore out and couldn't be passed on as easily. The cost of replacement shoes was simply not an option. Mick's father gave the problem his full attention and came up with two solutions. The choice was simple—bare feet or special shoes made by Mick's father. These special shoes were all custom-built and one-offs. Each of the children had a pair made especially for them. This seems to suggest that the family were not poverty stricken at all but there is more to come. The method of shoe creation was basically very straightforward and remarkably cheap. In fact they cost nothing at all except for the sweat and labour that went into the making of them.

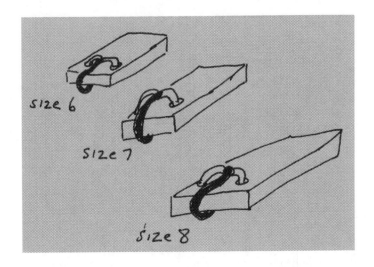

Each child was taken in turn and made to stand on a wide plank. The father, acting in his new found role of cobbler, then traced around the outline of their feet with a piece of chalk. This operation continued until the whole family had its footprints carefully traced out as rectangular images along the board. A saw was then borrowed and each image was cut out as best it could be. Cutting fine lines or curves in the boards was impossible; the saw could only cut in straight lines so the 'shoes' were hardly more than rough rectangles. Several holes were then bored through, by using a red-hot poker that was heated and reheated in the kitchen range; coarse string was threaded in and out through the holes to make the 'uppers'. Dr. Scholl had nothing on these. It wasn't only Mick's family who had this customised footwear; in fact many of the local kids had to walk around wearing similar 'cloggies'. The shoes were really uncomfortable and tiring to wear but they did keep the feet off the ground. During the depression, before the war, Mick said there was always a 'clonk, clonk, clonk, clonk' as the kids walked the streets.

Mick never told me whether or not the children were able to run in their 'designer' shoes—probably not.

Their house was very run-down and dilapidated; it had very little furniture and few possessions. Anything that remained in the house for any length of time was there simply because it was impossible to do without it. Unnecessary items were traded in for cash at the local pawn shops. They always had pots and pans—they had to cook! These pans were few and all of them were battered with age and hard use. Luckily they had the range for cooking and, since they could always find scraps of wood from the docks, they were able to keep reasonably warm and do the cooking during the winter. They had no curtains so once again Mick's father improvised—he painted out all the glass panes with whitewash applied with a thick brush—he made a terrible mess but the panes were covered. This let in light but kept the 'nosey' neighbours from peering in.

Everyone was forbidden to touch the whitewash once the windows had been painted in this way. If the father noticed any scratches or smears he went crazy and beat them all up—especially the mother. Mick told me that his father would be fairly normal before he checked the windows—he checked them as often as he could. If he found a scratch he went into a frenzy—he was a maniac. It was a living nightmare for most of the time. When the children were very small they were never allowed to play with other children because Mick's father had strict ideas about that. He thought all the other children were the spawn of the Devil and he didn't want his little angels to be corrupted by them. Of course, Mick and his siblings were just normal children and they hated being excluded from the rest of the world. To overcome the whitewash barrier they devised ways of 'accidentally' making marks so as to be able to see out through them. They became very skilful in making infinitesimally small scratches that it was just possible to look through and see the real world. Inevitably, the children or Mick's mother would brush up against the glass and cause marks that removed the whitewash. Eventually, the marks would allow strangers to see in and Mick's Father would have to make good the damage. Slosh! Slosh! Out would come the brush and whitewash yet again. Between each repainting there would be several beatings for the wicked acts that the children had performed.

Mick also told me that he and his brothers found ways of playing with the local kids when his father couldn't keep an eye on them. They ran wild a lot of the time but as soon as he was around they became the little angels that he expected them to be. They became quite adept at leading a double life—it kept the beatings at bay. Being children and playing in the dangerous places like bomb sites inevitably made an impact on their clothing and they would often be caught out by a rip or evidence of dust. Mick's father had an eagle's eye for such evidence.

The religious views of the father didn't only make themselves felt on Sundays in Hyde Park. Mick's father was a fanatic and he brought his religion into the household and made everyone else join in and suffer—you certainly weren't on earth to enjoy yourself. He wrote religious text and poetry and really fancied that he had a direct line up to God. He thought his poems came straight from the horse's mouth so to speak. Having written a great deal of the stuff, he decided one day that it was very selfish of him keeping it to himself—oh no! He should share his gift with everyone he could. He needed a way of promoting his ideas more systematically so he decided to build a prayer machine. This construction would enable him to focus upon what he really wanted to say and also it was a way of forcing his wife and children to follow his teachings about the glory of God. Their recitations would ensure the salvation of their souls.

Such was the poverty that building his machine could have proved beyond his means but the ways of the Lord are mysterious and Mick's father moved in mysterious ways and soon found a way. The solution was straightforward and only required readily available materials. He took: a cardboard box with one section partially removed to make a viewing window, a broom handle cut into two parts and a roll of plain wall-paper. In his best scrawl he wrote his own prayers, poems, psalms and scriptures. According to Mick, the things he wrote were adaptations of text from the Old Testament. The New Testament was not considered to be severe enough; Mick's dad was partial to 'an eye for an eye' or 'burning in damnation'—he didn't want any of the 'forgiveness' stuff.

Once the wallpaper scroll was finished it had to be mounted into the prayer reader chassis. The scroll was fastened at each end to a section of broom handle. The two cut-down handles thus became spindles for the roll; it meant that it could be read as the paper was slowly turned by hand and pulled across the open slot. It was a 'bodge-up' but I'm sure God understood. On wet Sunday afternoons, when he wasn't able to get up to Hyde Park, he'd drag out his holy machine and treat the family to an afternoon of worship—oh how they looked forward to that! Unless it was a child's turn to read, they had to sit in silence whilst dad read the words of God.

Grant Shorfield

There was a local vicar, who used to call round every so often, and once, serendipity smiled on him; he arrived just as the reading started. He was invited to listen and, of course, he thought it most admirable and laudable that the gospel was being actively practiced and promoted. The father's preference for the Old Testament rather than the newer, more humanitarian one was rather obvious. The vicar sat and listened but he was soon somewhat bewildered and disturbed by the nature of the words he was hearing. He obviously hadn't heard them before and their content was, to say the least, confusing. Squirming, the priest sat and listened and expected perhaps five or six minutes only. He had to stay a couple of hours in the end, despite all his efforts to leave. All his excuses of urgent business elsewhere meant nothing to Mick's Father. The vicar left with his soul badly tormented and in need of more conventional doctrine. He didn't call to the house again after that. He was the lucky one. Mick and all the other kids had to continue to put up with it. They hated it but were powerless to do anything. They had to sit around and all take turns. They couldn't let their minds wander because the father used to suddenly stop the reader in mid-sentence and expect someone else to carry on from the next word. If they didn't repeat it correctly, they were beaten for not paying attention. He certainly believed in "Spare the rod—spoil the child". He did his very best to make sure that the children were not spoiled.

Everyone would read, but eventually, one of them wouldn't be able to bear it anymore. They would turn one of the handles too quickly and this would tear the roll. The Father would leap at them and pummel them to the floor. Even so, he'd then have to spend some time repairing the damage and this meant a breather for everyone. It was worth a beating just to stop reading the damn thing. The rolls became very tattered after all the 'accidental' ripping. They were copied out in full once more with added verses and the revised edition was put on the roll. This suffered the same fate eventually and it too had to be abandoned.

As the children became older, so the repression became greater and greater until in the end, it reached the point where something or someone had to give. A couple of older brothers escaped by joining the army but Mick was still too young to escape in this way. The father was quickly losing his reasoning powers and his fanatical religion was completely taking over his reasoning. His tempers became more frequent, more manic and brutal and he would fly off the handle at the least provocation. The household was terrified of him. One day he snapped and went berserk. He was so enraged that he lost all control of himself. He was screaming in rage and grabbed the nearest child; he grabbed this child forcibly around the throat and started strangling one of Mick's brothers. The brother's face went crimson and the poor soul went limp in the tight grip of the murderous hands. It was obvious that the child was to die unless someone did something drastic. They were all trying to release the hands but were having no success. Mick's father was a man possessed and his hands had the strength of a demon—rather ironic really. Eventually Bill, another brother, picked up the small hatchet that was used to chop kindling for the fire. With all his boyish strength, Bill brought it down onto, or rather into, his father's head. The hatchet went straight through the scalp—making a new parting of his hair—before it lodged in the brain of the father. A look of bewilderment and consternation fell across his face. He released his grip on his son's throat and then stood up straight; he put his hands to his head and felt for the weapon lodged into his scalp. He pulled at it and finally he yanked it out; he collapsed as a jet of blood shot out splattering those present. Mick's Mother cradled his head while a doctor was sent for. It looked as though he was off to meet his maker; probably a good thing for all concerned.

The doctor came, applied himself to the unconscious victim. Mick's dad was carted off to hospital where, to everyone's surprise, he survived. He didn't get back to 'normal' though; an examination showed that the father had been suffering from a huge brain tumour, which the hatchet had cut through incidentally, and his peculiar behaviour was more easily understood. The father never really recovered from the incident and was a different person afterwards. He soon degenerated into a cabbage-like state and had to be institutionalised. It was never known if it was the tumour or the hatchet blow that finally killed him. Bill's action had saved the life of his brother but it also meant that he had shortened the life of his father. Well, what can you say? God moves in mysterious ways. Maybe, even God had had enough of the rantings.

With dad out of the way, the family became more friendly and open. Bill, the axe wielder, was taken away for a psychiatric examination by the authorities but he was released very soon after; it was obvious that the blow he had delivered was done solely to stop the murderous intentions of the father. Without Bill's action his brother would have died. The role played by the mother was never made clear to me but it seems that Mick never really got on with her. The family were abused by the monstrous father and had been long before the tumour played its part.

With the maniac of the family living elsewhere, life was simpler but even harder—now, there was no bread winner. Somehow, the mother managed to feed, clothe and care for the children on her own. Mick was fed up; he just needed to escape the dreadful life and now, there was nothing and no-one holding him back.

I did see his mother but only on one occasion. Mick had left a trunk at her house and he wanted it back. Mick asked me if I would drive him around to where she lived so he could collect his things. He hadn't seen her for about five years, even though she lived only a couple of miles away from him. He knocked on her door and, after several knocks we heard odd noises; we heard her coming to the door. She had the door secured by a chain and she screamed at us to go away. She sounded like one of those terrible women portrayed by the Monty Python team. Mick spoke calmly and told her who he was but she denied even knowing him. He persisted until eventually she went into the kitchen and peered through the window at us. Vague traces of memory flushed across her face as she saw Mick. She came back to the door and again asked him who he was.

Mick repeated what he had said earlier, and after much deliberation on her part she let him in. She refused to let me in at all. I had to stand back from the door so she could make sure I didn't try to sneak in with him. He went in and chatted to her for a while but she was totally uninterested in anything he had to say. He made his way to the room where his trunk was and I could hear her screaming at him not to steal anything from her. He found his trunk and asked her if he could get me to help him move it. She went off the scale and he realised he'd have to do it himself and so he started dragging it across the floor. It took him ages to get it to the front door. Even then he still had to pull it outside by himself because she didn't want me near the place. No sooner had he got it out of the door than she slammed it shut. There was no word of goodbye or anything, just a solitary slam. I could hear her talking to herself as she wandered around inside. I asked Mick why she was so horrible to him but he couldn't say. He did mention that she had terminal cancer. She was a very pitiful old lady. How awful that she seemed to be going along the same path as Mick's father. Mick and I struggled with the trunk and made our way along the balcony and down the stairwell to my car. Mick had suggested using his scooter for the collection but the trunk would never have fitted onto it—although, I'm sure Mick would have found a way.

Mick's family was only known to me through his recollections but I was lucky in that I also met Mick's brother Bill. He was the one who performed the surgery with the hatchet. He had done well at school and had grown into an accomplished angler; he was an authority on sea fishing and his illustrations feature in many angling textbooks and magazines. We drove over to Bill's house; Bill lived on the edge of a sprawling estate of sixties housing. We could have been in Croydon or Roehampton or anywhere else amongst the sprawling estates of London. Bill's house was one of the last to have been built; it backed on to a wood that led to a large open stretch of land that was ideal for walking. Bill was married; he had a couple of pleasant children. His wife, Mary, had at one time been Mick's girlfriend. Mick had met her whilst he was in the Navy and he actually planned his exit from the Navy to marry her. Mick had adored her and Mary had agreed to marry him when he had finished his service and got out. Unknown to Mick, his brother Bill got in first whilst Mick was still sailing the oceans. Bill asked Mary to marry him instead and so she did; she didn't want to wait for Mick's return. Despite this act of disloyalty there was still a great deal of affection between Mary and Mick. This became very obvious a little later when we all went for a walk.

Mick and Mary walked along together and Bill and I walked along behind them with the children. Mick was speaking at great length to her and she was joining in enthusiastically with his conversation. I got the impression that, had they been alone, they would almost certainly have jumped into the bushes for a quick one or two or three. Even I, in my youthful naiveté, could sense something was going on between them. Bill was much cooler towards Mick and even asked me what I thought of him and why was I his friend. Initially, I could feel his suspicions of me; it was perfectly understandable considering how badly Mick and Mary were behaving with each other. Bill's suspicions about me eased as we walked along chatting. I think he had met other friends of Mick and had not been very impressed by them. He had judged me in the same why before he changed his mind. He obviously had great reservations about Mick's visits. After the trip, Mick told me that he didn't really like his brother that much. It seemed to be mutual. Bill seemed to be the counter balance to Mick's eccentricity but the behaviour of Mary was confusing. Why had she seemed to respond to Mick's attentions so openly? It must have been painful for

Bill to witness her behaving so attentively to Mick. Had she married the wrong brother? I don't think so but that only became more apparent as I grew to know Mick better.

Mick suffered very badly with a serious condition and initially I was totally unaware of it. One day he came to me and 'confessed'. It was very embarrassing because he started speaking about his 'complaint'—he was so embarrassed. I immediately thought he had a dose of the clap—and I thought it was amusing that he was so uncomfortable about it; he didn't seem to have any problem with other bodily functions. It did occur to me that there may very well have been several other people, of both genders, who might share the same fate. Mick was not suffering from a venereal disease. He went on and on and in the end I told him to either tell me what the mysterious problem was or shut up. This inability to come clean and be honest recurred several times through our friendship. At last, having told me of his 'affliction' he refused to believe that it didn't affect me and that I thought it irrelevant to our friendship. He was afraid that I would think him weak and degenerate—he was that mixed up about so many things. I find it hard to believe but perhaps I was one of the first people he had 'got close to' who hadn't made a big deal of it. What was the problem—it was agoraphobia. I never really understood why he felt such shame about suffering from it but he felt the affliction deeply.

Having told me about 'the problem' I asked him how he managed to get around if he suffered as badly as he said. I was used to seeing him wandering around the local park or along the roads. I was interested in his solution. He said he had two methods. The first was his 'latching-on' method. He would wait at the exit of a building until someone else left in the direction that he wished to go. It didn't matter who they were; he would join them in conversation. He would then walk along with them until they headed off in the wrong direction and were of no further use to him. He'd then wait for a new unsuspecting guide and continue his journey. Eventually, he would have engaged enough contacts to get him to his destination. I'm sure he confused and worried a large number of people in this way. They must have been bewildered by the approaches of a stranger from nowhere who fixated upon them with irrelevant chatter and then left as quickly as he had arrived. It would have been interesting having a bird's-eye view of his journeys; they would have seemed quite odd.

His second method focused on the use of his bicycle or scooter. He was totally at ease in these ploys and used them to make all small journeys where it was impossible to latch on to somebody and walk. He was so clever at these antics that no one ever guessed he suffered as badly as he did. This explained why I had seen him riding his scooter across the school field for distances of fifty yards or less. On the scooter he was able to ward off the agoraphobia. Even so, I was sceptical and put him to the test. Once, early on in our friendship, I checked to see whether or not he was lying to me. My opportunity arose when we had to go to a bank in the local town. We went on his scooter and, after parking it, we walked to the local branch of his bank. I was about to go in with him when I made an excuse and said I'd wait outside for him. He went in alone and I waited outside but not in the place I'd said. Instead of being just outside the door, I hid in the adjacent doorway and waited for him to come out. He came out confidently until he realised I was nowhere to be seen. I had agreed to wait at the door. I wasn't there! He almost knocked down an old woman in his haste to get back inside onto safe ground. I nonchalantly walked into the bank and collected him from his predicament. I never said a word to him. I wasn't pleased with myself, I had made him very upset and uncomfortable—it was not the sort of thing I did.

CHAPTER **2**

We're all going on a summer holiday

My first conversations with Mick were in the May of 1967. I was a very gangly teenager approaching my sixteenth birthday. A couple of months later I was working in a factory that made model aeroplanes; I was doing a summer job. There were two reasons for this. Firstly I had no money and none was forthcoming from my Mother who had nothing to spare. Secondly, and more importantly, I was able to escape the confines of my family—it was my stepfather really—we loathed each other. I'd got the job in the factory because both my elder brothers had worked there and had created a really good impression; my sister-in-law was still there. I quickly learned what needed doing (5 minutes?) and settled into the daily routine. The factory was very old and dilapidated and in the summer it was stiflingly hot. I had agreed to work through the entire summer holiday; I was taken on to cover whilst other workers took their annual leave.

One day, as I walked out of the gateway, having finished work, I happened to meet Mick. He was driving past the factory gates on his scooter. He saw me as I waved to him and he pulled to a halt, on the other side of the road, beckoning me over with a wave of his hand and a big smile. I went across to him and we chatted for several minutes. He asked me what I'd been doing during the summer holiday and I told him about the factory job. I asked him what he'd been up to and he said he'd been working in a local park—he loved working with plants and had taken a temporary post for a few weeks. The conversation had run its course and we on the verge of saying goodbye when he asked me if I'd like to go on holiday to Cornwall with him. I felt slightly embarrassed; after all he was about thirty then and I was not quite sixteen. It did seem a bit odd that he should ask me something like that. I didn't know what to say to him. Even so, I told him to call round at my home later on and I'd tell him what I had decided to do. I gave him my address and he drove off leaving me to walk home alone wondering what on earth I had let myself in for.

He came around in the early evening and met my mother. After a short sociable, though strange, chat I told him I'd come, provided I could okay it with my employer. I went in to work the next day and saw the manager. When I told him what I wished to do he was really annoyed and started swearing at me; I was making it difficult for him. He had only employed me as a favour to my sister-in-law and he said I was really letting him down. The guy flipped his wig! I almost told him to stuff his job, but strangely, he suddenly calmed down, and changed his mood, and finally agreed that I could have the time off. With the benefit of hindsight I can see that I had put him in a very difficult position. He'd taken me on to cover for absent workers and I was proposing to absent myself at the time he needed me most. No wonder he was somewhat displeased.

In the short time between meeting Mick and the start of the holiday my Mother tried repeatedly to get me to change my mind about the holiday. She was looking out for my welfare and she thought it odd that a man, in his early thirties, that I barely knew was inviting me to spend two weeks alone with him in a distant part of the country. I only half-listened to her and decided her fears were all unfounded and decided I would go on holiday with Mick anyway despite anything she said.

I had about a week before the grand tour so I was to be able to buy a few odds and ends for the trip. Mick had tents, cooking gear—in fact; he had all the paraphernalia one needed for such a trip. I had very little to get myself. I bought a pair of jeans and a couple of tee-shirts and, if my memory isn't faulty, I bought a pair of baseball boots that

I loved. They were great to wear but had one unfortunate side-affect; boy!—they made my feet smell.

We set off on a Saturday morning in early August. It was clear and bright and I was really looking forward to the trip. The sunshine seemed to be a good omen and I was optimistic and expected to have a great time. Mick arrived on time on his 'bashed up' scooter. The previous owner of the scooter had attached a side-car to it but this had been removed before Mick bought it second-hand. It was hard to imagine that the scooter had enough power to propel a side-car as well. There was a hefty metal connector still attached to the kerb-side of the scooter. It was a large flange with four holes for the bolts that originally held the side-car in place. Mick could have removed the obstructing metal but couldn't be bothered. He had to sit with his right leg at a slight angle to avoid the metal obstruction.

Mick had already attached his items to the scooter and I loaded my bag onto the rear pannier and fastened it with a length of chord. I took very little—just a few items of clothing—there was no way of taking much anyway. Also, I knew I wouldn't be able to wash anything so why cart around a lot of dirty stuff. I had one problem; I was concerned about money but Mick told me not to worry as we wouldn't really need it. I didn't stop to think how we would manage to be away for a couple of weeks without spending money—ah, the innocence of youth. I had a little money saved from my work in the factory but hardly enough to pay for expensive holiday items. I needn't have worried—Mick didn't do 'expensive' so the problem never arose. We started off westwards but it soon became clear that I had no idea of what vibrations from a scooter engine do to the anal regions. After less than ten miles my bottom was a solid tingling mass of pins and needles. The seat of the scooter was very hard and I was wholly unused to it. The pins and needles hurt—they had gone well beyond the stage of discomfort. I kept asking Mick to stop but he was reluctant because we had hardly covered any distance at all. I must have been a 'pain in the arse'—oh dear, the awful humour has started. Eventually he stopped at a small grocery shop—he had to anyway so that we could buy a few things to eat later on when he planned to stop for lunch. The ride, after the stop, was even worse but I just had to grin and bear it. I missed much of the scenery because I had my eyes tightly shut as I endured the agony. It took about five days to get used to the vibrations—it was hell! On the other hand, when you start cycling after a long absence even a moderate ride makes you saddle sore. I was just a greenhorn as far as scooters were concerned.

The first day left us very exhausted from the drive. The constant vibrations even affected Mick. We didn't cover very much ground really but that was mainly due to the puncture we got in the front tyre. Almost predictably, this happened in the middle of nowhere. We were travelling along a very quiet 'B' road and passing vehicles were few and far between. We had no option; we walked five or six miles into a town to get the tyre repaired. It was a stark lesson to me. Walking five miles along country roads, when you are tired and hungry and thirsty, is a useful learning experience. I told Mick to buy a spare inner tube and a repair kit but he thought I was much too fussy and also he didn't wish to part with money unnecessarily. Finding a garage to repair the puncture wasn't a problem, once we had walked our way into the town. Unfortunately, we then had to retrace our steps to make our way back to the scooter to attach the wheel. The ten-mile back-and-forth hike and repair had wasted a big chunk of the late afternoon and it was early evening before we climbed back onto the scooter—ouch!—and set off again.

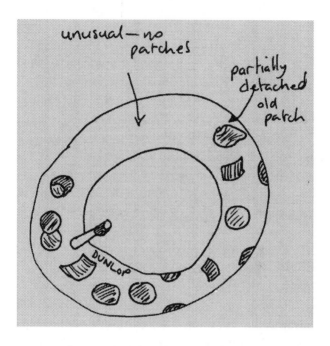

The picture doesn't really convey the dreadful state of the inner tube. There seemed to be more patches than original rubber; the patches overlapped and were pulling away as the adhesive lost its integrity.

I asked Mick where we would camp but he told me not to worry; there were lots of places for camping along the road. That may have been the case but Mick was finding it hard to actually find a spot that we could use. As we drove along,

Mick would keep stopping and suggesting ridiculous places to pitch our tent, one place was on a large front lawn, in front of a very grand house. He really had no idea at all but as evening fell we eventually found a spot. Actually it was an awful choice but, since it was rapidly getting dark, and we also had another puncture—this time it was a slow one, there was no other option. The campsite Mick chose was actually a small wood bordering the right-hand side of the road. The ground sloped away at a gentle thirty degrees (yes, thirty!) and we pitched the tent. The tent poles did their best to defy gravity at the angles they were standing—it was a scout's nightmare. We tied the tent strings to tree trunks and branches to keep the tent in position and stable. The wood was fairly young and mainly of hazel and chestnut so we were able to push it back or snap the branches to give us room for the tent. Even so the tent suffered from having numerous branches and twigs pressing down upon it. The tent lost its shape.

As the weather had been so sunny and dry, there was a plentiful and ready-to-hand supply of dry kindling, and more substantial pieces of timber, for our fire. The fire, once it was lit, was a little problematic as the embers tended to roll away down the slope. I solved this by placing a large piece of wood at the bottom edge to act as a barrier against the slippage. It also meant the fire was much larger than it needed to be—but, I love fires so it was no problem. We were not visible from the road but our smoke may have drifted.

In the semi-darkness, Mick rummaged through his packages and brought out a couple of enamelled plates, cutlery, a single, rather dented, aluminium pan and a kettle. From a bag he lifted out some canned food and I selected the beans. We had a meal of beans on toast—actually it was beans with toast. I did the cooking. It was 'charcoal' bread and overcooked beans that were little more than a paste. Our empty bellies didn't complain—we ate the lot. I used soil and leaves to clean the pan and the plates—the earth scraped off the remnants of the beans and a quick rinse in the morning would make the utensils usable again—or so I thought. After my fairly successful attempt at dishwashing we went straight to bed—there was no chance of a wash. I felt sticky and sweaty because I'd been made filthy from the dust in the air as we'd driven along and then I'd been made to sit in the smoke from the fire we'd cooked on. Isn't it funny? When you cook with an open fire it doesn't matter where you sit or where you stand; the smoke always blows in your face. Mick had also been in the same conditions but he seemed oblivious of it. Thus we settled down—tired and smelly. I felt and looked like a vagrant. Sleeping itself was dreadful. We both had sleeping bags; these had been provided by Mick and had seen better days. Neither zip worked, but since it was mid-summer, that really didn't matter too much. As I slid down into my bag I felt myself tumbling down the slope. I searched for support with my feet and managed to find a root to press against. The root support was fine whilst I was awake—I could focus on it. No sooner did I fall asleep than I felt myself rolling down the slope—my foot had slipped over the root. I adjusted my angle but as sleep crept upon me I found myself slipping down inside my sleeping bag and ending up in an uncomfortable position. Mick seemed to have gone out like a light. I tried my hardest to stay awake, so as to stop rolling down the slope, but I couldn't and drifted into sleep through sheer exhaustion.

Later on in the night I started having a most peculiar dream. I dreamt that someone was touching me; or rather someone was attempting to masturbate me. I began to have very erotic dreams about things one really does only dream about! This sort of dream wasn't that uncommon for me. I was in my mid-teens and I'd been having all manner of sexual dreams for quite some time—it was just a sign of the hormones that were now pumping around my body. I was quite used to waking after having a 'wet-dream'; it was just a stage I was passing through.

Strangely, this dream seemed very lifelike and I felt so much a part of it. The dream continued for what seemed to be a considerable time. It then ended abruptly as my feet hit against a root. In my squirming and turning I'd rolled partially out of the tent and down the bank. The root hitting me wasn't the only shock. I also found out that the dream hadn't been a figment of my imagination at all. Indeed not, quite the reverse. Mick was holding my penis and pulling me off. Dare I say I was terrified! I had not expected this sort of thing at all. I felt too scared to say anything and instead I tried rolling away from him. Each time I rolled he rolled as well and took up a new position alongside me. Despite all my pushing him away he kept on pestering me. Eventually, I had to tell him to stop. I said something like 'Leave me alone' and his hands withdrew. He rolled away and I felt a little less threatened by him. It didn't stop me from wrapping myself in a cocoon with the sleeping bag—I now wrapped myself in it right up to my head. I may have felt safer but I still felt very anxious and I didn't want to sleep; I did my best to stay awake so I could be on my guard but that was all to no avail; I was much too tired from the travelling and soon I slept from exhaustion.

I awoke with the early cool of the morning and found Mick was already cooking breakfast and making tea. He didn't say a word about the antics of the night and neither did I, until after we had eaten. I told him that I didn't want him to touch me anymore. I said I was prepared to continue the holiday provided he didn't try it again. He agreed but then he said he thought I was homosexual. I was astonished and asked why. He said he got this impression because of the way I walked. I was very pigeon-toed then. He apologised for trying to take advantage of me and agreed that he too wanted the holiday and was therefore fully prepared to forget any plans he'd had of seducing me. He said he wouldn't try to touch me again. I felt better after his guarantee but even so I wrapped myself up in a cocoon every night. This rather angered him but since it was due to his own foolish misjudgement he couldn't really complain. Fortunately, we quickly got over this little incident and the holiday started becoming enjoyable almost immediately. He did change my behaviour slightly though; from that moment on I did my very best to walk with my feet pointing outwards—I didn't wish to be caught out again. We pumped up the flat tyre and set off again in the morning. I sat further back on the scooter seat—I thought I needed a safety zone between us. Of course, as we travelled I inevitably slipped closer to him—but not too close!

safety gap

camping gear never normally stored like this

Our progress westwards was rather slow because Mick chose to drive down minor roads when the option was available. Actually, this was a much better choice because it meant we were away from the traffic and also we saw a great deal of the almost unspoiled countryside. Cruising along through the southern English landscape, in my naive state, I was lulled into a false sense of security about the mechanical nature of Mick's scooter. On our third day of the trip we had our first accident. We were going down a long, winding road that became a long gentle hill. It seemed to go on for miles and miles although it has probably been stretched by my memories. Mick was laughing and full of himself. The weather was delightful and we had no cares whatsoever to distract us. He jokingly told me that his front brake was not as good as it should have been. It was only meant to be a joke! The inevitable happened! The badly frayed front cable suddenly snapped with a loud pop. The back brake was hardly working at all—Mick and I knew that; it certainly did nothing to slow us down. We carried on with the downward slope of the hill having its impact upon us. Mick switched off the ignition and used the engine to act as a brake; it had no effect though as we accelerated down the hill.

I thought we would eventually stop but the hill had a mind of its own—as we turned each corner, so more road lay ahead of us—it just went on and on snaking downwards into the distance. Eventually we rounded a corner and this time, to our delight, we saw the end of the road in sight. Our road joined another at a 'T-junction'—we were on the leg of the T. Our jubilation was short-lived; it became clear that we were not going to be able to stop and we would end up going through the hedge on the other side of the road. I did my best Fred Flintstone impression and tried to use my feet on the road surface to slow us. Mick joined in with my futile action. We both dragged our feet to try to slow us but it was a waste of effort—we ended up in the hedge anyway. We crashed through it and fell off the scooter when we sailed out the other side. Fortunately it wasn't a prickly hedge—in fact it handled us rather gently. We dragged the scooter out of the field after the crash and Mick had a quick look at it to see if it was ok. There didn't seem to be anything amiss apart from the brakes. I looked at the front cable and it was obvious that it had been working on only a few strands before it had snapped. I had just assumed the scooter was roadworthy but from then on I always doubted Mick's judgment on things like that. Experience is a great educator. We restacked our belongings onto the rear pannier and then got back on the scooter and drove slowly on to the next town—with no brakes at all. Mick was sensible and he did take it easy but every downward incline caused me a moment of panic. We were lucky; there were no more big hills. The slower speed was good for me because the vibrations coming through the seat were very much reduced; travelling at a slower speed enabled my bottom to recover somewhat from the vibrations.

Accidents weren't our only holdup on our magical mystery tour. We also had a plague of punctures caused by Mick's own stupidity and lack of preparation. Both inner tubes were literally falling apart and seemed to be held together by the patchwork effect of the history of previous punctures. Mick diligently repaired the inner tubes several times a day but I thought this ridiculous and in the end he agreed to buy two new ones. He put the rear one in with no problem but the front one was punctured by accident as he slipped it on. Thus his brand new inner tube had its first patch. I was very sceptical of his repairs—the patches seemed to lift away after a short while (it was probably because the repair kit was so ancient and the glue had lost its ability to set.) The poor adhesive was probably working under duress caused by the tyres overheating from the excessive number

of miles we were travelling. The scooter was carrying two
people plus all the camping gear. No wonder the tyres got
fed up.

One puncture occurred in early afternoon. Mick checked
the map and we were at least fifteen miles from any town
and we were at a loss to repair it—having used up all the
repair kit glue. The offending wheel was removed and we
trudged off in the direction we thought most promising;
both towns on the map seemed very small and it was pot
luck if they had a repair shop. We tried hitching a lift but
the few cars that passed refused to stop for us. I'm not
surprised because we were incredibly scruffy by then. After
walking a while Mick, in his usual demure fashion, said
he was going for a slash. Jumping into the hedge he was
gone. I stood in the road waiting and waiting but he didn't
come out again. At first I thought he was having trouble but
remembering the first night I thought it best not to go in
to look. I thought he was playing a game to make me come
and find him and once I did he'd subject me to something
I didn't really want to do. Eventually he called out for me
to come into the wood. I refused and only agreed when he
told me his reason. He'd seen a large house that had a garage
and it would probably have the things we needed to be able
to help us get the puncture repaired. I was very reluctant
to try—I lacked the self-confidence needed to brazenly
walk across the grounds of a stately home and knock on
the door asking if they had a repair kit! Mick had no such
reservations and was soon off across the enormous lawn. I
ran after to catch him up. Together we went up to the front
door and knocked. I was very anxious and felt way out of
my depth standing in front of such an impressive entrance.
The journey across the lawn seemed to have taken minutes

and I had felt eyes on me all the time as I made my progress. No one answered our knock so Mick knocked again and this time we heard a response from inside the building.

The door opened and a country gent stood there looking at us. He was dressed in green and brown clothing and wearing wellington boots; he'd come through from the back of the house to answer the door. He enquired as to what we wanted. Mick asked for help and the man invited us in. He slipped off his wellington boots and slipped on a pair of slippers and led us through into a reception room. To my young inexperienced eyes it seemed very grand indeed and I felt wholly out of place. We were asked about our journey and Mick gave an edited version of what we had done and where we were heading off to later. For some reason the man really took to us and made us very welcome indeed. He asked us if we were hungry and when we said we were he took us in to the kitchen. We were given tea consisting of cakes, scones, jam and cream. It was incredible; we were having a cream tea for free. The man asked us for more details about what we were doing and together, Mick and I told him more about our drive down to Cornwall. He seemed engrossed by our tale and listened attentively. I noticed that though Mick told him more or less what we'd done he told it in a rather excessive way and made our journey sound very exciting. After we had finished talking we were taken to the garage and told to use whatever we chose or needed. The man then left us to it because he had to leave for a meeting. We were left on our own amongst a great deal of expensive tools and equipment that we could so easily have stolen. The large Bentley parked outside the garage would have made for a grand tour of Cornwall but we didn't run off with it. Surprisingly, Mick wasn't interested in theft. He had a noble character after all. We repaired the puncture in very pleasant surroundings with all the tools we needed and then we left. We walked along the drive when we took off—the man had asked us not to walk back across the newly seeded lawn that resembled a golf course. The drive meandered left and right and probably doubled the journey. Still feeling rather bloated from the unexpected afternoon tea, we fixed the scooter and continued westwards. What a day!

We camped that night and had a tough time of it. The rain poured down and we were soaked to our bones—despite being mid-summer the cold really seemed to penetrate right inside me and I thought I was probably going to be a future pneumonia victim. It was so bad that we got up at about five o'clock and headed into Southampton. We got into the town at about six o'clock. We both felt miserable and I really longed for a wash. Being so young I hadn't started shaving so at least I didn't need to sort out facial growth. Luckily Mick knew of a washroom from his days in the Royal Navy. I conjured up visions of the smell of soap, steaming hot baths, impenetrable steam and warm towels. I could see myself relaxing with warmth and clean smells. Reality was, as usual on this holiday, rather different. The building Mick took us to looked as if it had just crawled out of a slum and died. The roof was broken in and the whole place was run down and in need of repair. Mick wasn't bothered at all; in fact it was exactly as he remembered it. We parked the scooter and went inside. The conditions were lousy and one glance was enough to convince me that I would not wash there. Water was available; it was cold and dripped from a rusty pipe that was partially detached from the wall. The sinks were an evil shade of brown (not unlike excrement) and looked as though they could give you a case of dysentery from fifty yards. Mick was in no way put off and started his washing. He didn't use soap; he believed it destroyed the delicate biological balance of the skin on his hands and face. Instead, he vigorously rubbed the polluted water over his cheeks, forehead and neck. He then brushed his teeth—or rather he scraped them with his finger. It was horrible witnessing his foul manners and toiletry at that early hour. I was shivering and felt thoroughly miserable and was missing the more civilized comforts of home.

After his bathing was complete, he went into one of the cubicles to dispose of his number twos. Oh God! Some things really should be forgotten but the toilets burned their images on my retinas. The toilet cubicles were disgusting. A previous occupant had left his turds plastered onto the wall, cistern and seat. The occupant was obviously very generous because he'd also left some on the handle. I don't think I've ever seen such squalor and filth but Mick seemed perfectly ok; he seemed to be completely at home. He had a crap and then wiped himself with his hands because there was no paper. At this point I left—I couldn't stomach any more of it. I went outside and waited for him. It wasn't too much longer before Mick emerged 'fresh' and ready for the day. I was conscious of his hands as we walked along; at best he would have washed them in the filthy water; at worst he hadn't. It was slowly getting warmer as the sun rose up and very soon the sky was clear of clouds. The bitter chill that had gripped me was loosening its hold and I began to feel much better. As we were both ravenous we went into a café for a coffee and sandwich. I was horrified to see Mick calmly eating his sandwiches with his bare hands. The water, he may have washed in, had been filthy and yet he was calmly chomping away—he seemed blissfully unaware of the filth on his hands.

I was to learn a great deal about his eating habits during the course of the holiday. It was a wonder that he wasn't ill all the time or perhaps he had developed a superb immune system.

Whilst in Southampton, Mick decided to pay a visit to one of his old friends from his Navy days. The friend lived on the outskirts of the town and, since Mick had forgotten the address, we drove around for hours searching aimlessly. Mick could remember the house quite clearly and said he knew what it looked like. He was able to describe it fairly well but, for the life of him, he could not remember where it was. I became bored very quickly as the friend of Mick meant nothing to me; I had never met him and Mick had never mentioned him to me.

Still, Mick wanted to meet up with his friend and I was riding pillion so I had no choice but help with the search. Since I didn't know what we were looking for I was of no help whatsoever. After much tedious touring, around the outskirts of the town, Mick was all for giving up; it seemed to be a lost cause. Then suddenly Mick pointed at a landmark he recognised; at last he knew where he was. He had found the place. Mick parked the scooter and we climbed off. We opened the metal gate and walked up the path to a rather nice thirties-style house. The garden was well-maintained and the house in good repair. The house was in a very desirable location, fairly near some very attractive woods. The horse chestnuts, in particular, were looking their very best in the mid-summer sunshine. After all the time we had wasted on the search it seemed that fate was smiling upon us at last. My spirits lifted somewhat although I was very aware of how shabby we looked.

Mick knocked on the door. We waited and eventually heard footsteps approaching from inside the house. An unsavoury looking man, about Mick's age, opened the door and answered our knocking. He was about six feet in height with a pronounced beaky nose. He had black hair that was held in place by Brylcreem. His head shone as the light hit it. I didn't like what I saw. There was something really unpleasant about him, something that rather scared me. Unfortunately, he reminded me of my stepfather who also used huge dollops of Brylcreem on his hair. Being of the hippie mentality, Brylcreem was anathema to me.

He gave us both a rather perplexed look as he took in our appearance—he clearly didn't know us. It seemed he was about to tell us to go away but then he recognised Mick and his face beamed into a broad smile. We were immediately invited in. Mick showed his diplomatic approach as soon as we were in the hallway and he asked if we could have breakfast. I felt the blood rush to my face as I became embarrassed by Mick's rudeness but his friend was delighted and asked his mother to prepare something for us. We sat down and started chatting and the friend pumped Mick for facts about what he'd done since they'd last met and what was he planning to do in the future.

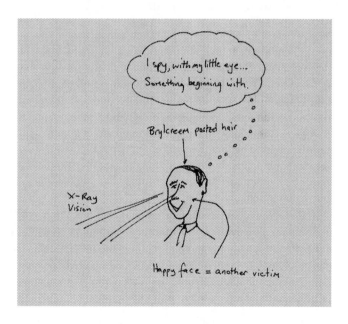

Breakfast was served and the mother joined us. She only joined in the conversation by asking our names. We told her. She listened attentively as we chatted and then frowned.

She then asked our names again. Puzzled, we told her again. This time she looked happier. The conversation carried on and once again she asked us both who we were. Again we told her. This happened at least half a dozen times. I was completely confused by it but Mick's friend explained the reasons for it afterwards. He told us that she was rapidly becoming senile and her memory was playing awful games with her. At times she didn't even know him—and he was her son! A little later, I wished that I hadn't known him but my reasons were not due to loss of memory—they were due to self-preservation; I didn't wish to be near him at all.

After breakfast we were taken out in the friend's car for a tour round the town and countryside. The car was rather luxurious—possibly a Humber; it had a high quality leather interior with a bench seat at the front. The trip was quite enjoyable for a while but then started becoming unpleasant. I was sitting in the front, next to Mick's friend, and every so often his hand would 'accidentally' fall upon my knee. I kept as far away as I could, but his 'accidents' seemed to happen with increasing regularity. I kept out of the conversations and listened to Mick and his friend reliving old times. Unfortunately, I became very uncomfortable because there were hints and suggestions about me. Mick's friend was too familiar and said how attractive I was and how much he liked my hair. It was obvious he had intentions towards me; I didn't wish to reciprocate at all. I was in a dilemma. I wanted nothing to do with him but, he was Mick's friend and he had been very generous when he fed us, so I had to go along with it as best I could and just be on my guard. I endured several hours being seated next to the predator.

The tour of Southanpton ended with us all going to a restaurant in the main centre. Mick's friend almost got into a fight when he tried to park the car. He had seen a free slot and positioned his car to reverse into the space. Mick's friend had driven absolutely correctly; he had indicated in good time and made it clear that he intended to park. Out of nowhere, a small vehicle slipped straight into the slot thus robbing him of the space. He climbed out of the car and I witnessed my first incident of road rage. I thought there was going to be a fight. Heated words were exchanged but it stopped at that. Voices were raised loudly but no blows exchanged. Mick's friend seemed to enjoy the experience. I didn't like it. I had to endure the meal with him as he acted lecherously towards me and I spent most of my time avoiding eye contact. The meal eventually ended and we left to go back to the car.

I was still safe and had avoided whatever plan he had for me. On the return journey I sat in the back of the car leaving Mick to grab the front seat—that was a tremendous relief. When we got back to his friend's house, I asked Mick if we were leaving soon; he suggested we stay there the night but I had no desire to do that at all. I said that, since I thought it was a camping holiday, I didn't want to sleep in a house. I could see I was causing problems but I knew what the alternative would be and didn't want it. Mick finally agreed, though very reluctantly, and we left to make a camp in the nearby wood. Inevitably, it was so dark that it was impossible to erect the tent; we slipped into our sleeping bags and simply pulled the tent over ourselves to act as a cover in case it rained. Once again, exhaustion was a great friend and I fell asleep immediately.

We woke early and were drenched from the sea mist that hung heavily in the still, morning air. We brewed tea and then packed our stuff onto the scooter. We were planning to head back to the friend's place—Mick wanted to say goodbye before we left. Unknowingly we had camped on the edge of a municipal park. I suppose we should have guessed because the grounds were so well maintained. We packed up the tent, and the rest of our belongings, and set off. As we drove across the well-kept lawn area, a man, who had been lurking in a hut, rushed out and demanded an overnight fee for camping there. Mick didn't stop but argued with him and refused to pay. The attendant got very stroppy and, to shut him up, Mick drove straight at him. The attendant dived to one side and landed in the soggy grass. We both laughed and tore off; Mick opened up the throttle and we raced off. We could hear the muddy official screaming behind us as he threatened to call the police. He may have called them but it certainly wouldn't have done him any good because Mick had no license or tax and was untraceable. I'll explain that later.

Arriving back at his friend's house, Mick suggested I walk to it by myself whilst he parked the scooter. I asked why he wouldn't come with me and he made up a stupid excuse about having to fix a problem, that he had just noticed, with the scooter. My self-defence radar kicked in; I knew something was up and I refused to go. In the end, despite some more requests that I turned down, he went himself and I waited at the scooter on my own. He came back a few minutes later. I could tell he was in a foul mood. I asked him what had happened and he accused me of ruining the holiday. I asked why and was told that he had arranged with his friend a liaison of sorts—for the friend and me. Since

I had refused to go to the house alone his friend had been done out of his part of the bargain; the restaurant meal had been a 'reward' given to Mick for serving me up on a plate. I was horrified. This was about the lowest thing Mick ever did towards me and yet, I didn't overreact or lose my cool. I remained quite calm. I must have had tremendous confidence in myself but I really don't understand why I didn't go home there and then. For some reason, I took what Mick had tried to do as something best forgotten and told him we should still try to get on with the holiday. Even so, I never quite felt at ease and was fearful of another encounter along the way. Mick was completely okay for the rest of the holiday and made no more advances or plans to sell me off to the next bidder.

After a few hours had passed and we were more relaxed with each other, I asked Mick about his friend and found out that they had been 'rather close' whilst in the Navy; Mick still saw him every couple of years or so. Unfortunately Mick's friend was a predatory fellow and his actions and attempts to pick me gave me a somewhat jaundiced view of gay men—on the other hand, I was only sixteen and I had plenty of time left to get over it—which I did. Mick's friend was vile and his sexual orientation was irrelevant—he would have been equally dreadful if he were heterosexual.

Mick and his charming friend had almost got themselves into very serious trouble on the ship they had sailed on. They were both able seamen and their duties were fairly boring and mundane with little responsibility or interest. Amongst their other tasks they had been working in the stores and had been given the task of cleaning and restocking it. As they went about their duties they had to visit many parts of the ship that were usually none of their business. On one such trip they discovered a storeroom containing large bottles of silver nitrate. As soon as they saw the word silver they decided that they would steal it and try to smuggle it off the ship when they had their next shore leave. They thought it must be very valuable indeed and would be a great trade in any port. Mick had a way with keys and was soon able to acquire the necessary set for the locked door. Mick and his friend let themselves into the store undetected and were able to steal several large bottles. They hid the treasure in a convenient place and looked forward to a lucrative future. No-one was likely to miss a few bottles and they'd be laughing all the way to the bank—or, more likely, some seedy dive in a foreign harbour.

Unfortunately, their scheme came apart when an announcement was made that the theft had been discovered. The nature of the incident was so severe that the Captain of the ship was notified. An intense investigation was soon underway and all hands were being questioned and checked. It became clear that the theft of the silver nitrate was deemed so important that there would be a court martial for the perpetrators when they were caught. The mood of the ship was foul as the officers set about their task and all the crew suffered longer duties and fewer privileges—somewhat like a prison—well, that's what the Navy did to maintain discipline—especially when it was dealing with ratings like Mick and his friend. The felons realised that capture was imminent so they decided to cool things down. They put the silver nitrate somewhere where it would be found. The return of the items sent a signal through the ship but even so, the investigation continued and it was some time before the ship's normal status was resumed. The silver nitrate was

critical to water purification and its theft had put the safety
of the crew in danger; unknowingly, Mick and his friend
had committed a very serious crime—had he been caught
he would have been severely punished. His guardian angel
(devil?) was looking out for him.

Despite Mick's attempts to introduce me into the sex
slave-trade we did eventually make it to Cornwall and spent
several really good days there We had a grand tour simply
moving from one small town to another; this was just before
the tourist attractions of the area were recognised by the
population at large. I saw many of the most beautiful places
as they were before tourism had its inevitable impact upon
them. I had never been down to this part of the country

before and I found the place delightful. We visited lots of the small towns and went onto many of the un-spoilt beaches; it really was fabulous as the weather was good most of the time. One of the best places was Mousehole—pronounced Mouzle—this was a tiny harbour town with a small fishing fleet. It was picture postcard stuff. We spent a couple of hours simply enjoying the place; it was very relaxing. We had the luxury of fish and chips for lunch. It was lovely; hot, clean food.

Other towns presented themselves in a very favourable light and then Mick suggested we complete the journey by going as far as we could. The furthest one could go was Lands End so off we set. When we went to Lands End the weather had turned from lovely sunshine to grey dismal rain—riding along on the scooter was grim, cold and wet. I suppose I was somewhat feeble but the miserable soaking I was getting did nothing to lighten my spirits. I was dressed in wholly inappropriate clothing and the wet penetrated through to my bones! When we arrived the weather made it one of the most uninviting times of that summer and there were very few people there. All the sensible people had stayed at home on that day. Mick and I were never the sensible ones. When we got there we discovered that it wasn't really much of a place to look at anyway and it certainly didn't register as one of my favourite destinations. Even so, it was the toe of England; so I felt compelled to travel as far as I could. I climbed down the cliffs and spent some time reflecting upon my situation; I tossed a few stones into the water as I looked at the vast ocean spread out in front of me. Being sixteen years old it was easy to be 'moved' by the spirit of the location even though the location itself was nothing much to speak of. Mick remained at the top of the cliffs and waited for me in the drizzle. The wind and rain helped convince me to leave so I gathered my thoughts together and climbed back up to join him and make our escape.

Camping arrangements were always very difficult on the holiday and they became even worse in Cornwall. Mick didn't want to use official sites at all and this was simply an act of meanness on his part. He didn't wish to pay for things that could be had for free. I tended to go along with this but it would have been much better if we had been able to have access to clean water and washing facilities. Mick simply found spots for us, but these spots were very difficult to come by; Cornwall seemed fully set against us. Lack of fresh water rather spoilt things and being thirsty became the norm. On our first night down in Cornwall, we had found no place to erect our tent and it was beginning to get dark. We were in the middle of nowhere and there was no moon. Mick did his best to find somewhere to help us out of our predicament but he had caused the problem himself. Eventually, he had no choice but to stop the scooter and we camped in a gateway to a field. The verge, running alongside the stone wall bordering the field, was only just a bit wider than the length of the tent when we had it set up. There seemed to be no traffic so we weren't worried about being run over in our sleep.

I put up the tent and made a fire whilst Mick walked off to get some water and wood for a fire. We had lost our water container earlier on in the day—it must have fallen off as we drove along. Mick trudged off, leaving me to do the fiddly work in the blackness of the deserted Cornish countryside. It was really tricky untangling the guide ropes in the dark, and then holding them fast with skewers that I pressed into the grass. The skewers were really difficult to use because they were twisted out of shape from numerous previous mis-uses. I made a mental note to straighten them each time I used them but somehow I never got around to it.

Mick was gone for ages and I began to suspect him of playing games again. I took a good look around to see if he was creeping up on me; I began to think he had some weird plan to leap out of the dark and attack me. My good look was really no more than a futile stare at the pitch black countryside. I could barely see my hand in front of my face. Recent events had certainly given me reason to be a little suspicious of Mick's behaviour. After perhaps an hour, he came back with a dented, rusty can that was nearly full of water but he also had his pockets bulging with apples and potatoes. These he had 'borrowed' from a farm across one of the fields. I made some tea and then prepared the evening meal, which was to consist of boiled potatoes and limpets which had been collected from the beach during the day.

The potatoes were easy; I didn't peel them—I simply boiled them in their skins until they were done. I emptied them onto a plate and used the same water for the limpets. I cooked them for ages and fully expected them to be edible; Mick had convinced me they were a delicacy and I would be surprised how good they were to eat. As we had been collecting them, I had wondered why we were the only people on the beach interested in them—surely everyone would be harvesting the delicacy. I repeatedly checked them for 'softness' but extra cooking time seemed to be having no affect whatsoever. I eventually gave up the idea of tenderising them and served dinner. The potatoes were stone cold now but tasted fine even though we had no salt. The limpets however were inedible. Though we chewed and chewed and chewed. The limpets refused to allow our teeth to cut them. It was like chewing large, tasteless lumps of rubber. Mick seemed to have more success with them but I imagine he was simply swallowing them whole.

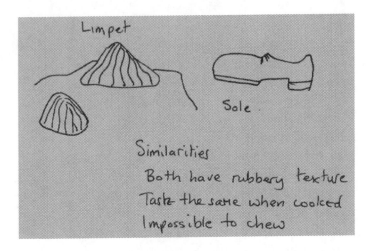

Fortunately, we had lots of bread and butter. I learnt another of Mick's peculiar habits when he spread the butter onto the bread. Not for him the use of a knife! Indeed not—he chose to pick up the butter and, with one smear, he wiped it across his slices of bread. Since the butter was soft it did spread quite evenly across each slice and yet the whole operation looked so coarse and uncivilized. I was much more refined as I used a knife to spread my slices. Mick thought I was very fussy and pernickety. After dinner he went out into the darkness to crap. He was gone for several minutes whilst he performed the necessary actions. He returned and immediately buttered himself another slice of bread. I asked him if he had washed his hands and of course he hadn't—I ate no more of that bread or butter and preferred to go hungry till late on in to the next day, when we went into town and I was able to buy something I knew was safe to eat.

We went to bed and fell asleep very quickly. Our days were long and the fresh air was taking its toll on us. Our fire slowly died down but its smoke was drifting gently across the road. Calm descended upon deepest, darkest, Cornwall and thus ended another day 'on-the-road'. Actually, the day hadn't quite ended after all. Very early in the morning I was shaken awake and immediately thought Mick was trying it on again. He wasn't, but the police were. Very roughly, they dragged us out of our tent and searched us. A dog stood by giving us affectionate little snarls every two or three seconds. We were questioned separately and had to prove our identities. I had nothing on me to show my identity but I was able to give them my home telephone number. They checked the details by ringing the number. My story was verified by my sleepy-eyed mother; she obviously verified that I was who I said I was. The Police relaxed a little but then they gave us a right balling out and told us to move on first thing in the morning. They had also asked Mick for his details. He gave them and they noted them down. They checked his scooter and cautioned him about riding it on the road as it wasn't taxed. They didn't know he didn't have insurance or a valid license. Mick told the policemen a story and surprisingly they accepted it and said it was okay for us to stay on for the rest of the night. However, they made it clear that we had to find somewhere official to camp the next night. They gave us details about where we could find official camp sites; we were told to just ask in the local towns. We gave our word that we would not cause them any more trouble and they left. Mick was very angry for the rest of the night and spoke about the police as 'bloody nuisances'.

The next day we went to the coast again and swam, sunbathed and just relaxed. The weather was very good and we really enjoyed ourselves. I was wearing trunks most of the time on the beach but Mick always wore his trousers, that he rolled up to his knees, or a pair of really horrible shorts that he'd kept from his Navy days. The shorts must have looked much more presentable when he was in the Senior Service. Mick suggested limpets again for dinner but I turned down his kind offer and suggested we eat something else i.e. something we could digest. We bought baked beans and sausages and some bread and this pleased me a lot. The thought of more limpets—well, it stuck in my throat. We had a great time loafing around but the afternoon peaked and, come the evening, I suggested we left early to look for somewhere to pitch our tent. Mick, in his own anarchic way, said we shouldn't worry as we had plenty of time and, since he was the driver, there was nothing I could do but accept the situation. We left the beach, as it began to get dark, and I knew we'd have problems finding a site but this certainly didn't seem to worry Mick very much, if at all.

We had a repetition of the previous night; we spent ages looking for somewhere to put the tent. After hours of looking we were still without a suitable location. It was getting irritating for us both because we were both very tired and our patience levels had worn thin to breaking point. Unbelievably, Mick decided to return to the place we had stayed the previous night. I was very much against this because I knew we were simply inviting trouble. As usual, Mick got his own way and he took us back there. I really have no idea why Mick felt so attracted to that particular camping site. Mick was the cook tonight and he did a great job of pasting the beans and burning the sausages. It is incredible what hunger does though, because we both ate heartily and ignored the 'bad' bits. Whilst Mick was cooking I pitched the tent behind the stone wall so that we were at least hidden from direct view from the road. I thought we might just get away with it if the police didn't bother to get out of their car. I had a tough time erecting the tent because the field had been ploughed recently; I managed to smooth down the soil so that we had a semi-smooth surface but the guide ropes were really hard to attach because the soil was so soft. The skewers would not stay in the ground and the ropes became limp almost immediately. I smothered the fire because I didn't want to draw attention to us in case the police came back. Satiated and tired it was time to sleep.

Once again, the tent was more a covering than a shelter. We rose to the challenge anyway and climbed into our sleeping bags. Luckily I had orientated the tent to run along the plough channels so we were able to place our sleeping bags in parallel ruts. We were exhausted and almost immediately we fell asleep. We slept but the long boot of the law once again interrupted our reverie. It was the same pair and they were bloody livid and I thought I was going to be dragged off to the cells and never be seen or heard of again. They had stopped the car, just in case we had returned, and there we were—ruining the Cornish countryside. Mick was very calm and somehow he talked them out of doing us for vagrancy, or whatever else was on their minds. Eventually, they left us but we were in no doubt that if they caught us again we'd surely be carted off to the local station to spend some time reflecting upon the error of our ways. Even Mick took heed if this advice and the next night he left plenty of time to find another site. I wanted to go onto an official site but he steadfastly refused this and wanted to remain 'independent'. I really don't know why the police had been so hard on us. We weren't really doing anything wrong; we weren't damaging anything—although Mick had stolen apples and potatoes I didn't think they'd have been noticed. I suppose we were just an irritation that the police didn't need or want and the sooner we were out of their hair the better.

The incidents with the police made an impression upon us both and we decided to move on. By now we had had enough of Cornwall and decided to head back eastwards on the leisurely drive back to London. Before we could start, Mick had to take a cutting from an enormous plant that we'd seen growing in a garden that we had driven past. Mick had an eagle's eye, when it came to spotting unusual plants, and he had almost jumped out of his socks in sheer delight when he'd spotted one specimen. Mick pulled over immediately and set forth to have a look at the plant and check it out. He did try to get a cutting the first time but the plant refused all his attempts; we only had a rather blunt carving knife that left the plant most unimpressed. After a bit of head scratching Mick realised that he needed something with an edge; he hadn't packed a hatchet so we set off in search of a hardware shop so that Mick could buy a suitable weapon to carry out the task at hand. Mick rose to the challenge and bought a small hatchet from a hardware store.

We spent some time touring around enjoying the countryside before Mick decided to head back to the plant and do what needed to be done. Oops, unfortunately Mick had not made a note of where the garden was and so we had to drive around and around most of Cornwall to find it. The roads all ended up looking the same and fulfilling our quest began to seem a lost cause. Mick was really upset; you'd have thought there had been a death in the family. He had really set his mind on acquiring a cutting. Eventually, he gave up, having decided it was a lost cause and what we were doing was a wasted effort, and so we headed off eastwards. There was another reason for calling off the search; the scooter was running short of petrol. I thought it most likely that our lost cause would leave us stranded in the back lanes. We had nothing to carry petrol in so we would have had to buy a jerry-can and then carry the heavy container back to the scooter. Our meandering took us miles away from any town. We were lucky; the petrol did not run out. Maybe the scooter was pleased to be going home at long last.

Not only did we not run out of petrol but lo and behold, about five minutes after we called it quits we went straight past the garden we had been looking for. The guardian angel was smiling down on Mick again.

Mick was ecstatic and stopped the scooter; fortunately his brakes were working now. Mick was all set to leap over the hedge to get a section from the plant. I stopped him by pointing out that there was someone working in the garden. This didn't deter him at all—he simply found a gap in the hedge and brazenly walked across the grass to the man. The man looked over, said hello and asked us how he could help. Mick returned the greeting, as did I, and then he went on to praise the enormous plant in front of us. The owner was very pleased by Mick's comments—the plant was one of his favourites and without our prompting he offered us a cutting. He then paused; he realised he had nothing with which to lop off a piece. Mick came in at that point and offered to lend the man his hatchet if that would help. The man remarked that it was very convenient that Mick had a hatchet—he didn't realise that that had been Mick's intention all along. Taking a spade the man uncovered a section of root and then set to it with the hatchet. It was hard going for the root seemed as hard as iron. The angle that the man had to chop through was also very difficult but eventually he chopped off a sizeable portion. Mick was really cheeky because he then asked if the owner had anything to wrap the cutting in. The man went to his shed and returned with a sack. Into this he poured some compost and earth and then carefully placed the cutting in so that the root was properly protected. He wrapped the root and then tied the top with a loop of string. Mick asked for some spare string so that he could tie the cutting onto the scooter. The owner was delighted to be able to help. He went to a great deal of trouble for us and even invited us in for tea but Mick surprised me by declining the invitation; he said we needed to be on our way. Mick accepted the plant gift, thanked him and then we left—Mick had such a knack of being able to manipulate people. He was so clever at getting what he wanted and in getting people to fall over themselves to help him do it.

The plant looked like an enormous rhubarb plant but I believe it was actually gunnera—a plant that usually only grows in large gardens alongside ponds or lakes. Mick managed to get it back to London successfully; he tied it onto the scooter along with his other treasures and kept the root ball moist. He was rather afraid that the leaves might get ruined by the wind but we weren't travelling fast enough to cause it any damage. When we did get back to London, he planted it in the perimeter of the school field and it took immediately and thrived. We both expected it to do well and it started to spread into a large clump. Unfortunately, weed killer was to be its downfall. It was a great shame. A few of the local lads broke into the school one night and poured weed killer over all the plants as an act of vandalism. Mick was very annoyed and upset about the loss of the plant. He took its loss personally.

On the way back to London we stopped for a last Cornish tea. The cafe we chose was situated somewhere on Dartmoor and was the only building for miles. The moor ran endlessly in all directions from it. From a distance, the cafe looked very picturesque and well worth a visit. We headed towards it and pulled up outside to have a look at it. It was very quaint and obviously not set up for the likes of us but this simply convinced Mick that we should try it. There was nothing better for him than the challenge of this sort of situation. He seemed to enjoy making middle class people feel uncomfortable. We stood outside in all our travelling roughness—hardly a sight for gentile eyes.

We were stared at as we entered through the door and the waitress, after a quick glance at us, rushed off into the kitchen; we heard her whispering to the rest of the staff. Several heads popped round the door to look at us. It was obvious that they felt we were most undesirable. Courageously, the waitress returned and showed us to a table. It was a corner table that meant we were screened off from all the other diners. As she walked away Mick chose to sit at another table, near the centre of the room and adjacent to the other diners; I joined him. The waitress turned around and there was obvious distress upon her face when she discovered us sitting in the wrong place. She decided not to ask us to move—she seemed to be really terrified. She brought a menu to us and stood there waiting very anxiously for our order. We ordered and she left to get it. It was served almost immediately, even though several other people were already waiting before us. None of them objected; in fact they were probably in on the unspoken conspiracy to serve us quickly and to be rid of us as soon as possible. I felt really uncomfortable but Mick was in his element. His table manners were even worse than usual and he seemed to make a point of talking in a very loud voice. The other people in the cafe were very quiet and seemed to be waiting for us to start something. They were really worried—perhaps they thought we were a couple of lunatics. The meal was very pleasant and it almost seemed as if they had given us too much just to please us. The scones were delicious and the portions of cream and jam were very generous. Though Mick ate like a pig, he took his time and the waitress was almost wetting herself waiting for us to leave.

Eventually we finished and asked for the bill. It came back almost the next second. We checked it and Mick noticed a mistake. He called the waitress over and told her about the mistake. Her face dropped as he told her of the error he had found, she obviously thought the 'trouble' was about to start. What sort of hell were we going to start?

In fact Mick showed her how we were being undercharged because she had missed off one item. She apologised profusely for her mistake and corrected the bill in the café's favour. Mick paid the correct amount and we left. Mick's honesty simply added to their confusion. As we left, there was almost a sigh from the building itself. We went to the scooter and climbed on and just before we pulled away we noticed lots of faces staring at us from the windows. Mick waved and blew kisses and then we left. The faces at the window turned red and hastily withdrew out of sight. On one level it was very comical; on another it was bizarre. I didn't really understand why we had caused them such a problem. Even before we had stepped into the doorway we were seen as a problem; our clothing and appearance was shabby but we behaved ourselves appropriately once we were seated—Mick was a problem as he ate so badly but that was just the way he did things.

Unfortunately, I think the cook had may have had the last laugh. I have suspicions that he may have doctored our meal and possibly added an ingredient that was not normally part of a cream tea. We had to stop about ten miles further on, because we were both overtaken by the most fearful case of the runs. We leapt off the scooter and chased onto the moor to relieve ourselves. It was horrible because the wind had picked up and our uncomfortable position was thus made even worse. It couldn't have just been a coincidence that we'd both suffered with runs simultaneously—I'm sure someone 'got' at us. After we had cleaned our insides out we had to do something about our hands. It was horrible. There was no way to wash our hands and in desperation I thrust them into the ground and rubbed the coarse gritty soil on them. At least the dirt on them was just dirt. We had to drive a couple of hours before we found a place to wash. It was an ordeal keeping my hands away from my face. Every few minutes I'd think about something else and my hands would inevitably move to my face and creep towards my mouth or my nose. I only just managed to catch them each time. I remember thinking I resembled a caveman—my hygiene was certainly something out of the Stone Age.

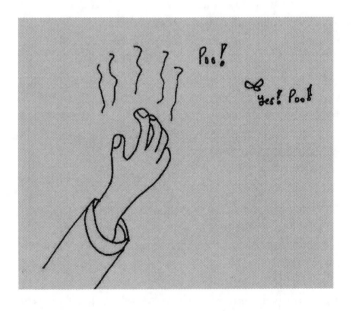

We deliberately came back to London using a different route so as to be able to see more sights. As we passed through Wiltshire, Mick decided we should go and see Stonehenge. He had visited the place several times in the past and he spoke very enthusiastically about it. En route, he and I fell out and were no longer on speaking terms. I can't remember what caused the problem but we travelled all day with not a single word passing between us—it was very juvenile on both our parts. We got to Stonehenge but I refused to even look at the ancient rocks—in fact I stared miserably in the opposite direction. Understandably, Mick left me in my sullen state and went off to look at the stones. My curiosity got the better of me and I soon succumbed to the attraction, it was marvellous and I rushed over to join him. We were able to walk among the gigantic stones and even sit upon them. This was a long time before they were fenced off to stop the Druids doing their stuff. I was astonished to see that people had carved their initials and thus had damaged the stones. Despite the gross vandalism the stones were incredible; so impressive and they certainly earned the fame that they have attracted. Our silly quarrel was lost as we wandered round the ancient site. I came away from there feeling most impressed by the efforts of those early Britons, as did Mick. We spoke about it and other sites as we drove off.

Since there were lots of ancient places on the way back we decided to stop and have a look at more of them. Some were nothing more than mounds of earth but even so their size was very impressive. I was amazed that human beings had been able to construct such enormous hills with the primitive tools available to them—what an achievement. It was an emotional experience wandering among the remains of the fortified hill. I remember trying to imagine how much effort it must have taken—I was overawed by it.

Mick decided we ought to head down to Lyme Regis. I had never been there and had no idea what it was like. The name sounded really impressive. I had heard of it but that was about the extent of my knowledge. When I saw it I thought it was wonderful. The Cobb, the named harbour wall, was a great attraction and we walked its length full of appreciation. Many years later when I watched the film 'The French Lieutenant's Woman' it brought back vivid memories of being there myself. We were there in wonderful sunshine rather than the gale suffered by Meryl Streep. For us it was simply charming and there was no hint of subterfuge or terror. We had great fish and chips—real food; we ate it looking out across the harbour as the small boats danced upon the water. Good Lord! I'm starting to wax lyrically but it was wonderful. Mick had really done well by taking me there. It was a high point. Mick knew of a wood to the west of the town and we set up our tent there and spent the night; it was a relaxed and uneventful night.

Whilst we were touring on Mick's scooter, the impact of the swinging sixties was making itself felt. It was the time when pop groups were making their 'concept' LPs. A couple of weeks before the holiday I had bought a copy of "Bookends" by Simon and Garfunkel. As we drove along I taught Mick all the songs though he was never able to learn the words or the tunes—a bit of a disadvantage where music is concerned. We drove along, singing at the tops of our lungs. I would start us off and he'd join in after a few words. He'd then turn to the front again so as to be able to steer. We'd both carry on singing independently but he always used to lose the rhythm and soon get way ahead of me. He would turn round every so often just to get his place again. Inevitably he would have to wait a few bars whilst I caught up to him. It was very amusing because I could hear all that Mick said or sung but my words were simply lost behind just like the exhaust smoke. Tiring of those songs, we'd sing Beatle songs, which Mick sang marvellously. He made them very differently from the original versions—in fact I often didn't recognise his peculiar and very personal interpretations. It was right at the start of the 'Flower Power' era and Mick was starting to go overboard about it all. Actually the singing was fantastic fun as we tore along across the rolling countryside. It was one of the nicest things about that holiday. Neither of us had a good voice but that didn't hold us back at all. Mick sang in his own little way but even so it was very amusing and entertaining. Since we spent so much time travelling, we soon suffered from dry throats, but even that hardly curbed our cherubic voices.

The holiday was nearing its end. Despite the god-awful first night and my moping around at Stone Henge, I had been having a really good time. We left Lyme Regis behind us and on the outskirts of the town Mick bought a couple of fish; they were to be our meal that night. We drove off into the countryside away from the business of the town. We were driving along a narrow, twisting road when we suddenly came upon a rabbit sitting in the middle of the road; it was taking no notice of anyone or anything. I had spent my very young days in the middle of Kent, The Weald, and I'd seen rabbits like this before. One look was enough for me to recognise the deplorable condition it was suffering—mixamatosis. As a child I'd seen hundreds of these unfortunate victims and I'd personally put quite a few of them out of their misery. The disease had been brought into the country with the intention of destroying the rabbit population. It was dreadfully successful and, since body lice transmitted the infection, it soon slaughtered the rabbit population. As the rabbit numbers shrank so the body lice were less frequently passed from rabbit to rabbit and fewer rabbits were infected; the disease struck an uneasy balance with the proximity of rabbit to rabbit. Rabbits almost disappeared from the countryside until decades later when they had evolved into a form with natural immunity. Mick the driver became Mick the hunter.

The rabbit that Mick had his eye on was in the latter stages of the disease. Its eyes were red, inflamed and had bloated enormously. It sat quite still, totally blinded by the awful affliction. I grabbed a branch, walked slowly and quietly up to it and dispatched it with a single blow. One of the eyes burst because of my actions—it was horrible. Mick was delighted by our catch, and decided it would make a good stew, and refused to listen to me and my objections. He really was going to eat it. I watched in horror as he took it to one side and started preparing it. He wished to skin it but he had to prepare it; he slit the belly to clean out the entrails. Suddenly he threw it down in horror. I came over to see why and saw that the inside of the rabbit's gut was alive with maggots. The unfortunate creature had been rotting away even before I'd killed it. Despite all that, Mick still wanted the skin from the 'mixie' rabbit to make a pair of gloves. I pointed out the simple fact that he only had skin enough for a single glove and also he had to cure the skin or it would go as hard as wood. My suggestion fell on deaf ears; my comments meant nothing to him. He simply hung the tiny pelt; along with two fish he'd bought in Lyme Regis, by a piece of wire above the exhaust. As we drove along, the skin was in a constant flow of the exhaust fumes. Mick had no idea really what he was doing. He hung the fish there to be smoked. He thought he was being very clever—perhaps he thought he was producing smoked salmon from the smelly herrings. The fish were not eaten; by the time Mick decided to cook them they had deteriorated so badly that even he was put off.

As our holiday progressed so the scooter became more and more like a travelling haystack. Apart from our luggage and camping gear, the scooter was also burdened down with numerous plants that Mick had lifted en route. I became very used to Mick suddenly stopping and jumping over the fence with a bag in one hand and a trowel or hatchet in the other. He became very adept at picking up plants in this way even if they happened to be in someone else's garden. He thought he was doing the plants a favour. He saw himself as a protector of plants and thus integrally involved in their distribution about the country. He was helping their proliferation and survival. Along with the plants, Mick had all our camping, sleeping and cooking items. Every flat surface of the scooter was hidden beneath a tied-on bundle.

Our appearance was also degenerating but, since we were so scruffy, it had reached a plateau. We were just about as untidy and smelly as we could get. We had slipped so far down the scale that we'd hit rock bottom. There comes a point when you can't smell any worse. I'm surprised the police didn't stop us. As cars passed the occupants would all turn and stare at us in disbelief. Mick and I simply smiled. One car stayed right behind us for ages whilst the occupants got an eyeful. The car overtook us and then slowed down so that the kids in the back of the car could also have a good look at us. It became too embarrassing being inspected at such length. Mick got fed up with it and had to pull over to the verge in the end simply to get rid of them. It was becoming a bore being stared at for so long.

Camping sites continued to be difficult to find and we usually ended up with a most unsatisfactory site. Mick seemed to have a knack of finding unsuitable places. One evening we passed through a part of Hampshire and simply couldn't find a place. Every time we happened upon a site we discovered a house or farm looking over it. We could hardly start a fire if we were in someone's front yard. It did seem as if we were about to have to travel through the whole county without stopping. Our gloom turned to delight; suddenly we came upon an ideal site. In the pale light, of an emerging moon, we stopped alongside a little stream, running alongside a grassy bank. We pitched the tent in the near dark and were soon fast asleep. We slept soundly and were uninterrupted by man or beast.

I awoke first and decided I needed a pee. I got out of the tent and stood next to a bush to relieve myself. As I did I looked around and suddenly noticed a footpath about five yards away. Swivelling my head, and almost soaking myself in the process, I saw a large house. We were camped on someone's front lawn! I rushed my urination and finished too quickly—I caught myself in my zip. In agony, I pulled the zipper down and untangled my foreskin from the teeth of the zip and then walked in a peculiar gate back to the tent entrance. Each step seemed to pull upon my damaged area.

I woke Mick and told him of our predicament and as usual he took it in a completely different way than I would have expected. He thought we were very fortunate—we would be able to go up to the house and ask if they would give us some water so we could make tea. I could just imagine the two of us, sitting on their lawn, with a roaring fire going whilst we had a brew up. Mick seemed to be serious, but

I didn't have his courage and prevailed upon him my fears and eventually, though somewhat reluctantly, he agreed to get up and move off before the household woke up and found us. Mick packed the stuff away and made no attempt to be quiet. I think he was being deliberately noisy. I kept expecting someone to come out and investigate at any moment but no one did and we were able to get away without incident. I wonder what the owner of the house thought of the mess we'd made of the lawn. He or she probably thought there were very large moles around. Maybe we were ahead of our time and were pioneers of crop circles!

Another night we camped in a field overlooked by a farm a couple of hundred yards away. Having no water—so what was new—Mick set out with our makeshift container to get some. We still hadn't replaced the lost one as Mick thought the cost a waste of money. Instead we were using a beat-up can. Getting fresh water was usually very difficult so I was amazed when he returned in just a matter of minutes. I was suspicious but even Mick couldn't pee that much that quickly. Being suspicious, I made sure we boiled the water to kill off any foreign bodies. It was relatively dark so I was unable to see what the water looked like. It was a dirty colour but Mick said this was probably a little mud that had been stirred up from the bed of the stream as he filled the container. After lengthy boiling I made a cup of tea for us both—it definitely tasted odd; I couldn't quite say what it reminded me of—I don't think I'd ever tasted anything like it before. I finished the tea and then gave in to tiredness. We scrambled into our sleeping bags and we went to sleep.

In the morning I went over to the stream where Mick had said he had got the water. The stream was an evil colour and smelt foul. I tracked back along the river until I came to the farmyard that we had seen the previous evening. A quick glance showed immediately why the stream was polluted. A trickle of urine and other delightful products was running straight from the cowshed into it. The previous night we had both been drinking diluted cows' urine. I felt myself retch but couldn't throw up—my stomach was empty. I went back to our tent and confronted Mick with this news and once again he thought I was very squeamish; he pointed out that since I had boiled the water I had nothing to fear; all the bugs would have been killed off so what was I worrying about. I didn't see it in quite the way that he did. I fully expected to die from plague or dysentery or more likely both. Mick had no such reservations and even used the rest of the water to make himself another cup of tea. He used the last of the water to wash his face. I really thought he was mad and told him so. He didn't understand my 'squeamishness—he really thought I was being much too finicky and namby-pamby. He told me I worried too much about unimportant things. Perhaps he was right but even so I still felt that he had no idea of how to stay this side of the grave—his habits were primitive to say the least! He'd have got on well with Cro-Magnon man—although that is probably a slur on our prehistoric ancestors.

The rest of the journey back into London passed without any real incident until we reached Guildford, just outside London. We were travelling along a main road and I was on the back of the scooter singing heartily, when the world seemed to go crazy; suddenly I found myself spinning through the air. It was very eerie. I was aware of myself tumbling slowly, and silently, through space and it seemed to take ages before I hit the ground. Reality and noise rushed back in an instant as I landed on my right hip and then bounced along the unforgiving road surface. I ended up as a tangled heap. My trousers were ripped through and my right leg was exposed and I could see it was very badly scratched. Grit and dirt was embedded into my calf and thigh. I stood up and gathered my wits together. I thought I was so lucky to have been uninjured. Then, the pain hit me and I collapsed with shock. A passing motorist had stopped and he threw a blanket over me while we waited for an ambulance. Mick was up and walking around—he'd not been hurt at all. He kept telling me to get up and get back on the scooter again. My carer told Mick to back off because I was injured. I could sense Mick's impatience with me. He had seen me standing up and so he knew there was nothing wrong with me. He was right. Apart from shock, abrasions and severe scratches I was as good as new.

Before long, I was carted off by ambulance to the nearest hospital and rushed through into the emergency arrivals area where I was given an X-ray. It took some time for the x-ray to be developed and I waited anxiously for the news. It was a tremendous relief when the x-ray showed that my hip was perfectly alright and I was therefore only bruised and scraped. I was given an anti-tetanus jab to counter the dirt that had scored my leg and then I was given a clean bill of health and told it was ok to leave the hospital—I was still feeling the terrors of shock and so I found this all very confusing.

I limped outside and Mick was waiting. He'd repaired the burst front tyre that had been the cause of the accident. I felt a horrible dread of climbing back on to the scooter and yet I really had no other means of getting back. I climbed on and prayed with all my might that nothing more happened to us. Fate smiled on me and we made the final leg of the journey back without incident. Mick did drive more slowly which I appreciated. At the hospital I had been given a long lecture on the necessity of wearing a crash helmet and I pondered this thought as we finished our ride together.

Grant about to eat gravel

Tyre in instant puncture mode

Mick doing Superman Impression

We got home in the late afternoon and I untied my small bundle from the scooter. I limped in to my front garden with my few belongings. Mick barely spoke to me before he drove off. My mother was very concerned about my limping but I shrugged it off and asked for a cup of tea. She made me one and then asked about the trip. I told her a shorter and censored version of all that had happened. She was both curious and suspicious but I refused to divulge too much—it would only have made her more anxious. I had to tell her about the accident and she was greatly upset and demanded to see the hip. I pulled down my trousers and as I did so I suddenly remembered I was wearing pants that had been on me for about a week. With great embarrassment, I showed her the bruise. By now it had really started to bloom and looked much worse than the pain I was actually feeling. It was enormous and highly pigmented, spreading right across my hip and down my leg. It also stretched about six inches up my back. It didn't really hurt much and I soon forgot about it and spent the rest of the day relaxing. My honeymoon away from pain was short-lived. The next day was absolutely dreadful. I found I was unable to move my right leg at all because doing so meant the most excruciating pains shot up my side. I rubbed in a tube of Deep Heat, which helped a little, but the rest of the day was spent feeling miserable. It took a couple of days before the pain left completely but the bruise was with me for weeks—it was that massive.

I went back to work at the factory on the following Monday and simply shrugged off the pain; being young made everything so much more bearable. I recovered fully and my bruise blossomed and passed through its many glorious stages. I didn't see Mick again during the holiday time and only met up again with him when school started again for me in September. I didn't seek him out; we just met by chance as I wandered the field again. Mick didn't seem that pleased to see me; in fact, he seemed rather fed up with me. I asked him what the problem was and he told me he had been sent a bill for the cost of the ambulance—he expected me to pay the bill. I was just seventeen and I didn't see it quite that way. The accident had not been my fault—it had been due to a faulty inner-tube repair undertaken by Mick. Anyway, Mick may have been a bit weird but he was the adult and adults paid the bills. I wasn't ready to assume such responsibilities at that young age.

Chapter 3

Mick at home

I'd told my mother and step-father some of the things that had happened and they both asked me to bring Mick around so that they could meet him again. They wanted to check him out and find out much more about the holiday. I had grave reservations about this but in the end I surprised myself and I agreed to ask him. As usual, Mick surprised me by agreeing to come around for a visit. I really thought he would turn down such an offer; he was still irritated that I hadn't paid the bill. He arrived on the designated afternoon just as we were sitting down eating a salad. He was shown in and, rather than waiting till we'd finished, he joined us at the table. We were all sitting with our lunch in front of us. He took the chair next to my young half-sister who was busily talking to her dad. My sister was so engaged with her dad that she took her eye off her plate.

Mick was talking with my Mum and as he did so he calmly took the knife and fork from in front of my sister and placed it in front of himself. My sister turned back to continue eating her dinner and saw an empty space where her plate had been. She looked at all of us and then at Mick—she had spotted a rat. She saw her things in front of him; he had calmly taken all of her eating items for himself and was all ready to tuck in. She said "that man's eating my dinner". It was a bit like Goldilocks and the three bears. We all collapsed with laughter because it really was funny seeing him eating her dinner like that. My mother got some more ham for my sister and Mick took some more himself as she held the serving plate too near him to him and he just dived in. He really took liberties.

No sooner had Mick left than I was pumped for more information about him. My mother asked if he had tried to do anything unusual on the holiday. I professed ignorance of what she meant; I played with her and tried to get her to be explicit—it wasn't very kind of me because my Mother was embarrassed. Did he touch you? Of course he did—we were touching all the time on the scooter. No—did he touch you 'there' (she pointed)? Oh no, of course he didn't, I replied. She dropped the subject but I knew she wasn't entirely happy and didn't quite believe me. She spoke to me the next day and asked me not to see Mick anymore. I told her this was impossible because he was my friend. Realising she wasn't going to get what she wanted, she asked me to be on my guard against him. I agreed almost too quickly which prompted her to ask why I should agree so readily. I blustered along in a hesitant manner and she seemed to back off again. Even so she knew I was holding back.

It wasn't until years later that I told her exactly what had happened. I explained why I hadn't said anything to her. I had known that she would have been very worried for my safety but I wasn't worried at all by what they had feared; I had been alone with Mick for a couple of weeks and having put him straight (an odd phrase to use!), he was perfectly okay with me. He never made any further attempt to seduce me or inveigle me into any tawdry plot. He took his interests elsewhere and I know of several other young chaps and young women he had his way with. I was always amazed to see how many blond chaps he engaged with—he seemed to be making a study of them. I must have fit his type in nearly all respects except for my lack of interest in him as a sexual being.

His women tended to come in all shapes, sizes and colour. Mick was not prejudiced in the usual sense; he didn't dislike anyone because they were black or Irish. He disliked most people because they were alive. I think his sexual preference was for blond males but he let his sexual appetite over-ride any restraint. What he didn't have was a normal relationship with anyone; he flitted around like a bee—pollinating where and when he could. Maybe he was infertile because he never told me of any problems with pregnancies. He never mentioned condoms—we'd have called them Johnnies—so he probably didn't use them. Unless his female companions were using their own protection he should have made someone pregnant. It didn't happen. Maybe Mick was firing blanks. That would have been truly ironic considering some of the things he was to say a little later.

Immediately after the holiday I saw very little of Mick. It was only after our discussion about the hospital bill in September that we had a new contact. From then on, I continued to see Mick on a fairly regular basis. He was still the grounds man but I didn't see him very much at school—this was deliberate. I was now on my A level courses and I really needed to focus on studying. I really didn't have time to waste hanging around with him during school time.

I usually went to see him on a Saturday morning. He had a flat about a mile from where I lived and this was stuffed full with his belongings and the odd items that he had picked up in his travels. One item of great interest to me was his modified music system. The tail-end of the sixties was a time of incredible change but we were all playing our records on really inadequate players. Mick's sound system was typical of the time—it was a red and cream 'Dancette' player. It was a box that was split across the centre to allow a hinged lid to be opened and closed. Singles and LPs could be played by placing them on a centre spindle and allowing them to drop onto a revolving platter rotating at the required 33.3 or 45 rpm. The output was through a single mono speaker at the front. These 'state-of-the-art' systems pumped out about 4 Watts of power (if you were lucky). If you turned up the volume to maximum you paid the price—the music was horribly distorted.

I was somewhat surprised by Mick's system; he had modified it rather drastically. He had added a box about six feet in length; the front of the box seemed to be made from an old red curtain and the other five sides were made of hardboard. A tangled electrical flex led from his Dancette to the box. When he played a record the sound came from his box rather than from the small speaker in the music deck. He showed me what he had done and I was very impressed. He had acquired half a dozen speakers and wired them together inside the box. They were mounted on a length of hardboard that had oval holes cut from it to allow the sound from each speaker to be heard. Each speaker was held in place by four bolts that passed through the hardboard and then through the mounting holes of the speakers. Mick had been very creative in his design. I saw nothing like this for several years until real stereo systems arrived in the early 1970s. Mick had discovered that you could put several speakers together, as long as they were connected in parallel. If they were connected in series the overall resistance was the sum of each speaker. So six speakers of 8 ohms would have offered a resistance of 48 ohms—the Dancette would not have been able to power that. If however, the six speakers were wired in parallel they still offered the same overall resistance and thus were compatible with his player. Unfortunately, the player could only pump out 4 Watts and this had to be shared through the six speakers—so the volume dropped. Even so, the quality of the output was much better than through his original system. He had created an early form of 'surround-sound' though it was purely mono-based.

For the majority of us, Mick's system sounded so much better than what we were used to and I copied his ideas for my own personal use. I had a transistor radio—it proudly exclaimed it had five transistors inside! The speaker was about two inches in diameter but it did have a connection for an ear-piece—it was a single ear-piece and it looked as though you were wearing a hearing-aid. I connected the earpiece to a four inch speaker that I taped onto the front of the radio. I also taped a huge 9 volt battery onto the back. The speaker and the battery dwarfed the poor little tranny that was sandwiched between them. The sound quality, although somewhat poor, was so much better than through the original speaker. The fact that I looked a 'plonker' didn't bother me at all.

Mick was really pleased with his music system and he told me about his earlier experience with music players. He had grown up and fell in love with the music of Caruso a world famous tenor who had died in the early 1920s—well ahead of Mick's misspent youth. Mick would often burst into song and out would come his interpretation of the glorious singer. Unfortunately, Mick's delivery was not quite up to Caruso's standard and, as I didn't know Caruso from Adam, I never recognised any of the songs. Mick showed me his collection of Caruso songs—they were all on 78s. These discs had to be played on an original wind-up player and he had one of these. He would often pop one of the Caruso discs onto the machine. He'd give the spring motor a few turns, engage the platter and place the pick-up needle onto the 78. As soon as the needle hit the 78 the scratchy music would burst forth. Mick was able to control the volume by opening or closing a vent that led to the enormous funnel that acted as the amplifier. The sound that came from the funnel was recognisable but the distortion caused by the scratchy sound noticeably depreciated the quality. This quality had been the norm throughout Mick's life and then suddenly, at the end of the 1950s a huge leap was made. Music was played on an electronic system that used electronic valves, rather than a huge funnel, to amplify the sound. There was no noise of a needle scratching the surface.

In our chats about his love of Caruso, Mick told me about the first time he had heard the sound of the new records that were being sold. He had been told by a friend about 'quiet' records and so he went along to a shop to buy one. He went into the shop and just asked for a quiet song—he didn't care what the song was or who was singing it. He just wanted to listen to a quiet record. He bought something—he couldn't remember what it was—after he'd heard it in one of the booths in the shop. Mick told me it was incredible. There was no introductory hiss; the music simply started as though the musicians were in the room with you. He could hear all the words clearly. Mick was knocked out by it and managed to scrape together enough money to get himself a player for the quiet music. Sadly, his Caruso collection was all on 78—his hero had long since passed away. Mick didn't lose his love for Caruso; he'd grown up with the scratchy sound and that did not detract from the pleasure at all.

A couple of months after we got back from Cornwall Mick decided to hold a party and I was invited. I'd heard about his parties from others who'd been to them—I was led to believe they were really 'wild' and so, being my usual inquisitive self, I was looking forward to it. I arrived a little late and was bewildered by the unsavoury looking characters already there. I thought I was in with a good chance of getting my throat cut before the evening was out. There were 'spivs', rockers, sluts, nutters, Religious nutters, Mick and me. I wondered which category I fitted into. I tried talking to several of them but I was either ignored or received such hostile looks that I thought it best to ignore them. I sat around on my own simply listening to the music and watching the light show.

The lights intrigued me—probably because Mick had slipped something into my drink when I wasn't looking. He was quite capable of tricks like that. I went over to have a look at how the light show worked and was shocked to see Mick's bodge up job. He had taken an old LP and stuck small strips of aluminium foil onto it. This disc was then placed on a record player turntable and set into motion. The pickup arm had been modified; the pick-up cartridge had been removed and in its place dangled several metal brushes with fine flexible bristles. A wire was attached to each brush and this carried mains current; every time a brush swept over a piece of foil a circuit was made and a light came on. Each strip of foil was contacted to a different light. The lights were of different colours and thus Mick had created a multi-coloured display. Mick's light device had three speed settings that matched the records that could be played; thirty three and a third, forty five and seventy eight. Mick changed the speed every so often just to add variety. The lower speeds were ok but when the machine was racing along at 78 rpm the sparks were a little too dramatic and Mick stopped using this frenetic setting. Had anyone fallen onto it or spilled their drinks there would have been a death. With the lights out it was eerie but very exciting seeing the shower of sparks jumping from his light machine. Perhaps the drink added somewhat to the appreciation.

Mick stopped the party at one point and told everyone that he was going to show some films. He had his cine projector set up and a white bed sheet the other side of the room acted as the screen. He showed the films that I'd seen previously in his shed. The Swedish woman washing herself went down fairly well but the films were too short (they only lasted a couple of minutes), were silent and were too 'tame' for the audience and Mick stopped the show before he'd finished showing all his collection. Mick was used to the films being very popular but he had changed his audience from fairly young teenagers to more astute and discerning adults—I use those words rather loosely. Everyone went back to what they were doing previously—sitting around, drinking, ripping off the heads of chickens (I exaggerate a little here), talking and snogging. I was on my own most of the time except when I managed to get Mick's attention but he was busy with his other guests.

Somewhat later Mick came over to me and pointed out the ugliest girl I'd ever seen in my whole life. She had a fairly good figure with slim hips, well-proportioned breasts and good legs. It was such a shame that her face let her down. Mick was dreadful and I was appalled by what he told me. He boasted of how he'd had her. He told me that he'd told her she was very beautiful, very clever and interesting. He deliberately took advantage of her. To top it all, he then asked me if I wanted a quick fuck with her because, if I did, he'd fix it up there and then. Fortunately, I had enough of my wits about me to turn down his very kind invitation—I may have been drunk, but I wasn't that drunk. Although I turned down his offer I felt bad about it. I felt guilty about not wanting to have sex with her. Was I turning her down because Mick was being so vile, or was it because she was so ugly? Being seventeen didn't help at all. Fortunately, I collapsed shortly after and didn't wake up until the following morning. I was very lucky that I didn't have a hangover. Mick and his ugly girl were already up and moving about and we cleared up the party mess together. The party goers had been very careless and had not bothered with their rubbish or cigarettes. There were many burns in the carpet where cigarettes had been dropped onto the floor and ground out underfoot. We cleared the mess and I used Mick's vacuum cleaner to suck up the dog-ends. The vacuum cleaner had seen better days and the hose kept falling apart as I used it. The connection to the body of the machine had long since admitted defeat and had dropped off. Even so, the dilapidated machine overcame the struggle and the rooms returned to their usual clean but cluttered state.

Mick's many artistic talents started at around this time. He was busily studying for his 'O' Level exams, which he hoped, would enable him to get into a teacher training college. 'O' Levels were sat by students of about fifteen or sixteen and were a prerequisite for continuing on to A Level exams or getting a 'good' job in a bank. He was expected to sit maths and English but one of his examinations was to be art and he spent a great deal of time and effort improving his skills. He did quite well at it. I came round to see him one day and he told me that he'd painted an enormous bird on his bedroom wall. I fully expected it to be a disaster—it wasn't. I was greatly surprised when I saw what he had done because it turned out to be exceptionally good. The completed mural was perfectly matched to the proportions of the wall and the painting itself was spot on. I'm not sure that I would have liked it on one of my walls, but even so, I had to admit that it was first-rate stuff. He hadn't asked his landlady, who lived downstairs, whether she minded the murals and I thought she would be livid when she saw what he had done. It was quite the opposite reaction in fact, because she was delighted with it and even commissioned Mick to do one for her. Since Mick needed the practice with his artwork, and the money would be very useful, he was quite willing to do as she asked. He painted an enormous jungle scene in her front room. It completely covered the longest wall and it took him weeks to finish. The landlady was in raptures about it and invited lots of her friends and neighbours in to see it. They all wanted Mick to paint one in their houses as well and Mick was soon inundated with requests to do similar Tarzan scenes in many of the local houses. He lost interest though and only did one more but he put all his efforts into it and once again this turned out as superbly as the two previous examples. His paintings were of an excellent standard but I always thought they should have been done on canvas or illustrations in a book. That was my prejudice and what do I know about art? I thought his birds resembled the images that adorned the Brooke Bond tea cards—I had collected these cards myself so I was very familiar with them.

I called round to see Mick one day, not long before we both went to college, and he told me he had a tape recording that he wished to play to me. He took out a reel of quarter inch tape and put it on his tape recorder. Mick plugged in the machine and turned it on. We had to wait while it warmed up. In those days all the music devices were driven by valves that needed time to warm up. If you looked inside a radio, a television or a music deck you'd see several red-hot glass tubes inside. We waited until the magic-eye came to life and changed from red to green indicating the machine was ready for use.

Mick flipped the switch to play mode and I waited to hear what he had recorded. There was a short lead-in of blank tape and this ended with a short blast of severe distortion;

he had obviously had the microphone turned up too much and created violent negative feedback. I knew there and then that I would be listening to something a little different from the norm. Eventually the noise settled down to a gentle and constant hum—the inherent sound of the valve amplifier. Finally, after a long build-up the recording started. I could hear people clapping and singing and praising the Lord. I listened for a few moments in silence and then I burst into laughter because it seemed to be a tape of loonies making silly noises. I thought Mick had either met a convention of mad comedians or he had visited a lunatic asylum. The recording delivered a constant barrage of religious screaming—a holy cacophony! At first it was very funny but it continued and continued. You can have too much of a good thing. I became bored with the noise but then my interest was regained; I recognised a loud voice shouting out—a voice that stood out from the rest—I knew that voice! It was Mick! Of course it was!

The noise died down and I heard Mick shouting the praises of the Lord. He would say something and all the others repeated it. A couple of songs followed and it was clear that there were no good singers present—it was horrible. (Perhaps they were trying to get rid of the neighbours.) I asked Mick what it all meant and he told me that he had gone along to a religious meeting with his girlfriend Rose—a Jehovah's Witness. Unfortunately, she was fairly slow-witted and Mick really took advantage of her. She lacked all guile. He used to make her stay the night at his flat and then, after sex, they would both say they were sorry. Then they'd both pray to God and beg for his forgiveness. Mick was a low-life rat about it, though; because he told me things she had done to him. He told me she went wild when roused and he once showed me her bite marks and scratches where she'd lost control. As usual, Mick soon tired of her and Rose was given the push; about a year later she died in a car crash. She had been badly injured and died from loss of blood. There had been no need for her to die because a simple blood transfusion would have saved her. The transfusion was refused by her relatives because of their religious beliefs. She died—that was the end of it for her. When he told me, Mick reported her demise as though he had barely known her. Perhaps that was how it was.

Mick really enjoyed attaching himself to lunatic religious groups, and sects, because they were all filled with eccentrics and nutters like him. Over a period of time he introduced me to some very disturbed people of one religious conviction or another. I was always on my guard when I met them. It was quite interesting really because Mick and I took very different views about these people. He seemed besotted by them; I found them naïve and contradictory. None of them had any lasting impact though and he soon tired of their company. I think he was experimenting with these people as he tried to take on board what was happening in society. 'Flower power' and 'free love' were terms bandied about in the media and Mick wanted his part of it.

The final days as grounds man at the school were very strained for Mick. He was continually in conflict with the teachers and the situation soon developed so much that the staff actually wanted the authorities to sack him. Mick really caused a bit of a storm by writing to the teachers and the Head of the school telling them that their educational methods were all wrong. This in itself was perfectly reasonable—we were living in a democracy and everyone had a right to their point of view, but Mick suggested preposterous alternatives and was very slanderous about the people he criticised. Also he never quite got his facts right. He would stand up for a fourth year thug and not bother to check the facts—he would present a case that held no substance. He would allow himself to be deliberately misled. The Headteacher wrote several letters to Mick's employer but nothing came of it; there seemed no way they could get rid of him. It seemed they simply had to wait until Mick left the job. They were delighted when they learnt he was set to go to college, although this was tempered by the thought of him being in charge of young people. They had their suspicions about him but had never managed to acquire any hard evidence. This seemed to be Mick's modus operandi—the mud never stuck.

Mick's conflict ended abruptly. Mick became involved with one of the sixth form girls. She was not exactly bright to say the least. She would return to school after the lunch break with lurid descriptions of how she had sucked him off in the pavilion. The story got around and eventually arrived at the Headteacher's ear. He now had a way of getting rid of the 'problem'. Mick told me that he was called in and confronted with the evidence of his deeds. Mick somehow turned the attack around and told the Headteacher that unless he was left alone he would tell the newspapers. The Head was in a jam because the girl was over the age of consent and Mick was not a teacher, so he wasn't subject to the normal codes of professional behaviour. This was a long time before any legislation had found its way into common law. They eventually worked out a compromise in which neither of them would say a word about it, but Mick agreed that he would no longer threaten the teachers as he had been doing previously. This resolution was put into practice and Mick dropped the girl like a hot potato. She really thought Mick was a lovely gentleman and was heartbroken when he stopped seeing her—he wasn't 'seeing her', he was simply taking advantage of her. Gullible wasn't the word for it.

Nothing more happened before he left except for an irritating little incident on the penultimate day. He had left his bike outside his work shed while he did some work inside. While he was thus engaged some thieving little 'Herbert' stole it, Mick was effectively trapped. He couldn't walk across the field because of his agoraphobia. Mick waited for someone to wander along but no-one came to his aid. He was forced to stay there the whole of the night. He wrapped himself up with old sacks, which had contained fertiliser. He was rescued in the morning when the first kids came across to the pavilion for orange squash. He latched onto one of them and invited the kid home with him. The kid agreed and went with him—or rather he took Mick home! Mick washed and changed his clothes and then returned to school on his scooter, which he kept his eye on for the rest of the day. Thus he finished at the school. Towards the end of my time in school I had seen much less of him, mainly because I was revising for my A level exams and I really couldn't afford the constant distractions upon my time. Revising with Mick around would have been a disaster. With Mick there would always be a massive distraction or disturbance. Life was never boring or steady.

Since we were both choosing teaching as a career, Mick asked why we didn't go to the same college. He had chosen one about a mile or two away but I was reluctant to attend a local college because I really wanted to leave home. My home life was unbearable and I simply had to get away. If I went to a local college I would have received a small grant and be expected to live at home. If I chose to go to a remote college I would get a much larger grant that would include money for accommodation and food. Moving away to college was the perfect solution. There then followed a brief breakup of our friendship, which lasted about three months. It was the summer of 1969. The Beatles had released their Abbey Road LP—John Peel had just started his Dandelion record company and I really liked the 'sounds'. Suddenly life looked bright for me.

Chapter 4

Off to college

My science teacher, Mrs. Thompson, had suggested I move away from home and attend a college at the other end of the country. I loathed my step-father and her advice, on this occasion, hit the mark and so I started applying for colleges all over England. My first choice was the teacher training college at Canterbury. It was not really the other end of the country but it was a step in the right direction. I took the long train ride southwards and arrived in the charming but strange town. Although I was from the south I had never visited Canterbury before, so it was an exploration for me. I walked from the station to the college following the instructions that I had been given. There was no problem at all; the map and guide were perfect. I arrived on time and was met by a panel of inquisitors—no! They were the interview board. They were very welcoming and friendly and were skilled in putting the prospective candidates at ease. After a brief welcome they asked me an easy question just to get the event started. They threw me an opener to get me relaxed before the interview kicked in fully. It was a breeze, no problem at all. They asked me how many brothers and sisters I had.

Now, this should have been easy; I should have felt fully at ease and answered their opening gambit with a simple single digit response. Oh, no! I had to make it hard for myself. Instead of just giving a number I found myself floundering as I tried to count up my siblings. Most people have their forefathers—I had a problem because I had four fathers. My mother had consorted with four men and several had produced children with her.

Counting up the various combinations was really tricky. As my mind was churning through the various subsets and combinations I knew I had blown-it—I could sense the looks of disbelief on the faces of the panel. Why on earth would they want to enrol a student who didn't even know how many brothers and sisters he had? It was no surprise that I failed that interview.

Spot the Dad Competition

Having been turned down by my first choice, my forms were forwarded to my second choice. This college accepted me without even bothering to call me for an interview; the travelling distance was probably the major consideration in their decision making. They just looked at my previous exam successes and accepted what my teachers had predicted regarding my A level exams. I was accepted and was given details about where and when to turn up in late September.

I had one problem. I had been going out with a girlfriend for about six months and I was very keen on her. She was somewhat cooler to me, but I served her needs at the time. She didn't like my family and she certainly didn't like Mick. My family didn't take to her and I was told I could do much better. My girlfriend was extremely clever but not a 'good-looker'—her looks didn't bother me too much although it did hurt when they made comments about her crooked teeth and large chin. She wasn't that bad—or was she? She came to my parents' house the day I left. She was very quiet and acted as though she was very upset by the prospect of me leaving. I had no reason to doubt that and left with that image of her looking sad and alone. On our last time together she had decided to wear a very short orange mini skirt. This was most unlike her normal mode of dress and my Mother found it very difficult not to stare at the knicker exposure that was caused when she sat down. I too was distracted and it helped make the ending easier. My own level of sadness was tempered by the experiences I'd had with my step-father. Living in the same house as him had been absolutely dreadful—but it was over.

I was free at last. My stepfather and his dreadful oppression were behind me. I caught the train northwards and was away. As usual I had left at the very last minute so everything was an awful rush. The train journey seemed to go on forever; I don't remember much about it except for a very long delay at Rugby, but eventually I arrived at my destination. I found the address of the place I was to stay at. It was a small place, like those houses you saw in the early episodes of Coronation Street and I found myself facing my landlady. She was okay but I did find it very uncomfortable when she started telling me all the dos and don'ts about living there. She had been somewhat surprised by my arrival. I had arrived holding a large cardboard box in my arms. I didn't own a suitcase and I hadn't been allowed to take one; my new 'father' had disallowed this. He had great pleasure in watching me walk down the road with my belongings in a box. I should have felt humiliated but I was so full of hatred towards him that I felt no shame. My new landlady showed me upstairs to my room. A fellow student had arrived earlier and had grabbed the larger and much better room at the front of the house; the front room was also better for a much more important reason but that will come out later. Having stashed my box of possessions in my room I made my way to college. My landlady gave a good set of instructions and I got to the college in only twice as long as I should have. Her route must have been the tourist special—it took me everywhere except where I really needed to go. Still, I managed to get some basic orienteering done as I meandered my way around the town and its outskirts.

As I approached the college I could see the tall blocks that formed the main college centre; I headed towards the towers. I arrived in the lawned grounds of the college just as everyone else finished the afternoon meal that had been specially laid on for the new entrants. I was too late to join in the meal so I had to go without. I joined the ranks of the other newcomers and, feeling very much on my own, I trundled along with them all to a meeting. I felt very intimidated because there were so many people there. I felt quite helpless and out of my depth. After the meeting we were told to walk around the college so as to become acquainted with the buildings and get a feel for the place; we were all given a rough plan of the college buildings. Knowing no one else, I trudged around feeling rather lost and forlorn. Fortunately, a young woman in her third year befriended me. She had seen me wandering around aimlessly and had caught my attention—she took me to her room and offered me coffee and biscuits. She told me how much she had enjoyed being at the college and she said I would have a great time of it as well. It certainly made it much easier for me and I was very grateful to her for her charitable act. I felt much more relaxed and left after the friendly chat and, to my regret, I never bumped into her again—it would have been pleasing to have been able to say thank you to her for her kindness.

I went back to my digs and met a fellow male student who was sharing with me. He was very 'straight' and seemed both astonished and appalled by my longish hair. He was the son of a rural doctor in Buckinghamshire and his beliefs and ideas were usually very traditional or bordering on the reactionary—to say the least. He and I didn't get along very well at all. He loathed my socialist politics as much as I detested his Daily Telegraph outlook.

My very first evening in my digs was awful. I woke up at about three in the morning—I really thought there was an earthquake. Actually it was the milk train—the first train through. My bedroom window was less than five yards from the railway embankment. It was very strange looking out of my window and seeing and feeling the rolling stock pounding along. My flat mate had chosen well—he'd taken the other bedroom at the front of the house so he was about ten yards from the line. The noise was overwhelming but, having no choice, I had to get used to it. Human beings are incredible. Within a few days I managed to sleep through the thunderous noise and vibration; I was aware of it but it didn't wake me.

Our digs were fine though; they were clean and the furniture was comfortable. Our bedding was cleaned on a weekly basis; this was a new experience for me because I was used to bed linen being changed when it got itself up off the bed and threw itself into the dirty laundry pile. The landlady had only to prepare us a cup of tea in the morning before we set off in the morning. All our meals were provided at college. This meant we had to get up at seven o'clock and walk a mile for food. Having very little money I had no choice but to walk in at that ungodly hour each day. Lunch was served at one thirty so missing breakfast was an absolute 'no-no'—a missed breakfast was unsettling for the rest of the day.

My flat sharer was called Anthony and he and I were at loggerheads most of the time. Mostly it came from the fact that I was rapidly becoming a more strident socialist and was therefore constantly arguing with him about his conformist and reactionary ideas. Also he was doing P.E. as his main subject and so he was constantly going on about the need for brutal exercise. Every morning he'd be up at six and then be off around the back streets of the town. At first I thought this very funny but he was really offended by my rather crass criticisms. In the end his running became a taboo subject, as did so many things. We agreed to not talk about the things we disagreed on—we didn't talk much after that. One thing he did that did interest me was canoeing, which I took up and became reasonably skilled at. I seemed to have a flair for it and soon I was much better than him—he didn't like that and actually spent a lot of his spare time trying to reverse this and become better than me. It was so funny because I only did it one afternoon a week, for a laugh, whereas he was having special tuition and exercises and was still doing worse than me. He never did catch me up.

I wasn't lonely for too long because I soon became involved with several activities that really helped me socialise. One girl in my mathematics group had problems with the work and we used to help each other out—it was no more than a study session but at least I had someone to talk to. Also, several of the canoeists were splashing around in the water for the same reason as me—just for fun. We formed a small group of recreational canoeists and we tended to socialise together. We'd go to the local pub for a game of darts and a drink.

Every Saturday night there was a live band and a disco. The bands were playing cover versions of the current hit records. One band was particularly good at performing copies of Creedence Clearwater Revival songs; I remember a really good version of Proud Mary. I attended these discos on my own and I didn't really enjoy the first couple as I had no-one to talk to. I thought I should become a bit braver; I liked the look of one girl I saw dancing and braced myself and gathered the courage to approach her. I asked her to dance and, since she eagerly agreed and then held me rather tightly, I stayed with her during the rest of the evening. Afterwards, I walked her back to her digs. We kissed—it was very nice—I enjoyed it. I felt on a high as I walked back after my first 'snogging' session at the college.

As I walked back to my digs the elation gradually faded and I began to feel some pangs of guilt; I had my girlfriend back in London—I suddenly missed her. I rang her the next day and expected to have my spirits lifted, but instead I was deflated. I sensed that she was feeling somewhat cool towards me and the old cliché of 'out of sight—out of mind' filled my thoughts. I felt I had been disloyal to my girlfriend so I thought it best not to have any contact with the 'disco' girl again—I was rather timid. The next day my disco date looked me up but I acted as if nothing had happened (it hadn't really anyway—had it). I took everything very coolly. She was rather surprised at my indifference but didn't say anything. She was talking to me amidst a group of girls she was staying within one of the dormitory blocks. She left but her 'friends' stayed and I continued to chat to them. I got on quite well with them and we used to meet in one of the common rooms at lunchtime. My disco girl became friends with other students and our paths didn't really cross very much after that.

Unfortunately, another one of these girls took a fancy to me and that was the last thing I wanted. I tried ignoring her attentions and pretended I wasn't really noticing her at all. Eventually, one of her friends came up to me and, in confidence, told me that her friend had spoken about how much she fancied me. I explained that I wasn't interested in her because I wasn't really interested in anyone at that time. She reported back to her friend but it didn't work and I still found myself the subject of her actions. After a couple of weeks of this I decided to speak directly to her about it. As I introduced the subject her eyes lit up but it was clear that she misunderstood what I was saying. She thought I was about to ask her out. Eventually as my words hit home and she realised she was onto a loser with me. Suddenly, she turned everything on its head and told me to get lost. She said she'd never been interested in me and failed to see how I could have jumped to that conclusion. She was very 'offended' and stormed out. She told her friends something unpleasant about me and I found myself shunned by them.

A few weeks after I arrived at my new college I began to suffer with a toothache. It was one of the upper molars on the right-hand side of my mouth. At first I had no more than a dull sensation but within a few days the pain began. My landlady was very sympathetic and offered oil of cloves that she swore would do the trick. It was a little helpful but the pain was only inhibited briefly and came back with a vengeance. Aspirin was totally useless. I was advised to go to a dentist. This was a problem for two reasons; firstly I wasn't registered and secondly I expected to have to pay for the treatment (in fact, as a student I would have received free treatment). I endured the pain but it only got worse. It reached a crescendo one night and I spent long hours wondering what to do with myself. I had to get a solution. I decided to go to a dentist and asked my landlady if she knew of one. She told me about the one she used and I went along.

I had no appointment but the agony I was suffering helped me get treated; I was told to wait until a free slot came up. I was there for a couple of hours before they squeezed me in. The dentist took one look at the tooth and told me that he would take it out. In 1969 not much thought was given to 'saving' teeth. If they were a problem they were ripped out forthwith. I was given gas and welcomed oblivion as the pain disappeared. When I awoke my mouth was awash with blood from the gaping would where the tooth had resided. I felt a bit groggy but all the pain was gone. The discomfort of the wound was nothing compared to the dreadful pain I had endured. The dentist showed me the tooth and it was clear I had been suffering with a massive abscess. I rinsed my mouth several times and then had to write a cheque for the treatment. I was shocked by the cost of the 'private' treatment but it was a small price to pay for the benefit of being pain free. As I walked home I couldn't help my tongue exploring the crater in the top of my mouth. I now had a gap where a tooth should have been. It wasn't pretty but it was a whole lot better than living in agony. Now, when I hear of someone suffering with toothache, I tend to be sympathetic to the sufferer—I've been there; I know what it's like. I did take better care of my teeth afterwards and brushing regularly became the norm.

I had another dramatic experience at my digs. Anthony and I were allowed to use the front room downstairs as a study and we decided to make it more comfortable by having tea and coffee. Our landlady only provided breakfast and would not allow us into her rooms to make drinks. I bought an electric kettle; it was a major expense for me and also a leap up in convenience. I had been used to kettles heated upon stoves and electric kettles had been nothing more than a pipedream or something seen in American films. I bought the kettle and was delighted with it; it heated the water in no time at all. Anthony provided the cups and we shared the purchase of instant coffee and powdered milk—yuk! I still hate that stuff. The kettle worked really well and it provided the two of us with drinks on demand. Our taste of luxury was interrupted rather rudely.

I came back from college in the late afternoon and my landlady spoke with me as soon as I got in. She berated me for almost causing a fire in her front room. I had no idea what she was talking about. She took me in to the room and it smelt horribly damp. In the centre of the room, sitting isolated in the centre of a small table was my kettle. Instead of looking shiny and gleaming it looked dull and tarnished. I picked it up and peered inside; the electric element had fractured! My landlady told me that she had seen smoke coming from under the door and thought the room was on fire. When she went in the room she found it full of steam. She said I had left the kettle on when I went out. She was right; the kettle had boiled dry and, as there was no cut-off, the element had overheated and burnt out. I told her I hadn't used the kettle that morning; I knew this was true as I had been late getting up and was rushing to get to my first lecture. Anthony must have left the kettle on by accident. She didn't believe me and the incident rather soured our relationship.

I asked Anthony about the kettle and he vehemently denied doing it. I knew it wasn't me, my landlady was most unlikely to have staged such a scene—it must have been him. Anthony and I barely acknowledged each other after this. I checked out the price of a new element but it was almost as much as a new kettle. In those days shops did not provide replacement parts as readily as they do now. I left the damaged kettle in the front room; my first taste of class had been so short-lived.

I didn't like the college experience very much and showed little enthusiasm for the lectures and work. There were two reasons for this. Firstly, I had the girlfriend in London and missed her a great deal. Secondly, I really didn't like the P.E. mentality of so many of the students. Come the first half term, I had decided to leave the college one way or another even if it meant giving up teacher training. I went to my personal tutor and said I had to leave. He was a little hostile at first and asked for my reason; I blurted out a long and complicated lie about my stepfather. I said he was close to dying of lung cancer and my mother had written asking me to come home to help her in her hour of need. How could I refuse her request for support? My personal tutor was very sympathetic and I got in to see the Principal soon afterwards.

An appointment was made for me by my tutor and I went along in good time. I met another student who was also wishing to transfer from the college. He went in first and came out after a short time looking thoroughly deflated and humiliated. His request had been turned down and he had been told to buck his ideas up or leave altogether. He was told that his lack of commitment to the college was noted and he would be checked to ensure he kept up with his work. He was given a really nasty time of it. He wished me luck before he walked off looking totally crestfallen—I began to doubt the success of my mission. Fortunately, my 'reason' for leaving was based upon real facts. My 'step-father' really was close to death and had been whisked off to a sanatorium for treatment of pneumonia. When the Principal asked me what the problem was I had a catalogue of facts that supported me. I only left out one detail; I didn't tell the Principal how much he I loathed my step-father—in fact, I was delighted he was suffering.

As I was telling my story, he listened attentively and sympathetically and agreed it was best for me to return to London to be with my family when they most needed me. He told me to reconsider quitting college altogether and instead get a transfer to a London college. I did feel rather bad about having misled him but my reasons were without malice. Yes, they were for personal gain but they were not for greed or self-advancement. I took his kindly advice and, during the October half term I went to visit a college near to my family home. My task was simple; all I had to do was ask if it would be possible to arrange a transfer. I retold my story and was provisionally accepted. I was told to get formal permission from my first college to allow the transfer to go ahead. The Principal of the first college was already sympathetic so I had no problem at all in getting the approval I needed.

The college I transferred to was very close to my parental home and, although I didn't know it at the time, it was a college supported by a religious institution. This meant that alcohol was forbidden and they really meant it. Several people were suspended for having booze in their rooms. I had no idea that my new college operated an alcohol free zone; in truth, it wasn't a big deal anyway because I didn't really drink very much; I would hardly be missing something that I didn't even use very often. My mind was focused upon other affairs. Two issues were foremost in my mind. Firstly, I was near my girlfriend again, and secondly, I happened to know someone who was a student at the new college.

Chapter 5

Mick's room in college

Whilst asking if it was possible to transfer to the new college I stated that I knew Mick. The Principal actually knew him very well. She knew him well and was on good terms with him. I was really surprised that she knew Mick; Principals of colleges didn't really get to know the names of the students. It certainly made my entry into college easier. Things were going well and she surprised me again when she sent for Mick. We were halfway through the interview—Mick had no idea that I was there seeking a transfer—she just wanted to let him know what was going on. He came in and gave a huge smile when he saw me. There then followed a very informal chat session between the three of us—it was all very easy and relaxed. I was made most welcome. I did have to travel north again to wind up my affairs at the first college. I really didn't want to go but I had to sort some things out. Anthony was very surprised when I gave him my electric kettle. He didn't know what to say; he took me for a drink and we had a game of darts. Our time together ended pleasantly. I was taken out to a Chinese restaurant by my canoeing friends; they treated me really nicely—I had second thoughts about my transfer but the deed was done.

Mick had a room in college and since I knew no one else, I tended to gravitate towards it when I first started at the college. As Mick and I resumed our friendship so his room became an obvious focal point. It was an incredible place because, unlike most students who make do with half a dozen books, a record player and a couple of records, Mick had a vast amount of personal stuff littering the room. From the ceiling he had suspended his huge glass chandelier. It looked comical surrounding the measly 60W light bulb. One wall was completely taken up by a bookcase that Mick had brought with him. The shelves were packed with books of all descriptions and topics. There were a large number of books on botany since this was his major interest. There were also books on religion, drugs, health, medicine, history, science in general and also his prized works called 'The Encyclopeadia of Sexual Perversions'. These were large, grubby, red volumes that took up about two feet of shelf space. Every possible perversion imaginable was carefully described and illustrated in these works of human accomplishment—I know because I checked it! Mick claimed he found them in a dustbin and since they were such 'good' looking books he thought it a great shame that they were going to be destroyed. He was doing humanity a service by saving them from the fire. Mick had put many of his belongings into storage in the large attic that ran along the entire length of the building. That attic was to prove useful to Mick a couple of years later.

In all the time Mick was at college he read only one book, despite the fact that he bought a large number of them. His single reading experience was that of a rather second-rate book on child psychology that even then was years out of date. He bought two copies of every book whilst at college.

One copy was for reading, which he didn't do anyway, and the other copy was for displaying on the shelf. He had a bizarre way of reading and no doubt this accounts for the fact that he read so little. He would pick up his book and open it no more than 30 degrees so as not to break the spine. This meant that his books stayed in excellent condition but they also stayed unread. His bookshelves rapidly filled up with two copies of everything.

Mick had another horrible set of portfolios, which consisted of photographs taken of mutilated bodies that the police had had to deal with during their investigations. Each photo was accompanied by a lurid passage describing how the various mutilations were caused. They were the worst books I've ever seen in my life but he thought they were 'educational'. He had found them in a dustbin, behind a police station, and had liberated it for his own benefit. He never told me why he was looking in bins behind a police station but, strangely enough, it was not in the least unusual for him. I just took it as fact.

One thing was true about all of Mick's books; all of them, except the sexual perversions were totally unread. Mick collected them with enthusiasm and thought that the mere possession of them would somehow put all the information into his head. Reading books was for fools as far as he was concerned.

The rest of the room was cluttered up with clothes, which overflowed the ridiculously inadequate wardrobe. Electrical equipment littered the floor: there was an old electric typewriter that gave you shocks if you typed certain keys too hard, a couple of large and rather monstrous statues, a stack of silver service trays and serving dishes—many items that were not really those that defined a student. He had his old record player that now seemed to have low fidelity; he had disposed of the speaker box because there was no room for it. He wasn't careful with records and I was always scared to lend him any of my records to play on it.

Actually, I did lend him two records. One was a copy of Paul Simon's Songbook. Mick thought this was quite good and he lent it to another student. This student lent it to another. When I discovered what Mick had done I had to track down my record. I went from pillar to post until I got it back. It had ended up on the record player of the president of the student union. My new record was now scratched and worn and the cover was badly bent and damaged by coffee cups being placed upon it. I wasn't too happy about this. The other record I lent him was 'Ask me no questions' by Bridget St John. Mick was amazed by this record. I really liked her music but Mick thought she was magical. He said her music would be remembered long after Paul Simon was forgotten. Mick's prophecy didn't work out very well. He particularly liked the song that mentioned 'buttercup sandwiches'. Fortunately, Bridget St John was a minority taste and the record didn't leave Mick's room. When I got it back it was still playable although it had several scratches on it that Mick had created for me. Every click and hiss is a gift that sounds just the same today as it did when Mick put it there back in 1970.

Mick's clothing was very shabby. He had several pairs of really scruffy, down-at-heel shoes. He really knew how to dress badly; he was skilled at this from his toes upward. He wore odd socks—why not? His jacket had pockets that were dreadfully baggy and bulging from holding too many personal items. Mick always looked scruffy. His shirts had collars that were worn badly through many years of use. He had two jackets, one of leather and one of corduroy, and a long heavy-duty winter coat. The coat was ex-military and he had got it from his time in the navy. It kept him warm but it was not much of a fashion statement. Despite the hippie fashions dominating the young (and not so young) Mick never really took to the floral designs; his clothing was rather middle-aged even though he was in his early thirties.

He had one item of clothing that he was especially proud of. It was a suit that he had designed himself, whilst serving in the Navy. He had been stationed in South Africa for some time and decided he needed to improve his wardrobe. He drew up the sketches of the suit and took it along to several tailors. He was refused by them all. When he was posted to Asia he tried his luck again and this time he was rewarded in his search by finding a Chinese tailor who would be delighted to undertake the task; Mick had finally found a tailor with no scruples. I'm not surprised at all that the tailors had grave reservations because the suit was so awful that it is impossible to describe accurately. The words: 'awful', 'what a mess', and 'oh my God' spring to mind. The thing just didn't look right. The material was a light blue and grey check design—it looked wrong for a suit. Another major defect was the waistline that had been placed to run just under the shoulder blades. The trousers were a crumpled mess. The crotch seemed to be all drawn up on itself. Mick put the suit on and showed me how he looked. He spun around expecting me to be equally impressed by his fashion show. I wasn't! Mick thought he looked fantastic and, rather than spoil his illusion, I kept quiet about it. He never wore it outside the room because he had always been laughed at whilst wearing it. In the Navy his shipmates had taken the 'piss' something rotten but Mick still thought he was right and everyone else had no taste.

He also had a large silver serving set. He used this to great effect the evening he invited all his main lecturers, the Principal, Vice Principal and other dignitaries on the college staff to his room. He gave them a splendid meal, which they all thoroughly enjoyed and the evening turned out to be a great success for Mick. Of course, all the students, me included, thought he was a right creep doing that sort of thing, but Mick never gave a damn about social conventions and the what not—which I suppose was quite courageous. His serving dishes took up a whole corner of his room. I have no idea how he managed to get them all into his room or how he managed to prepare a large meal with the minimal kitchen facilities available to him. As ever, he was resourceful. Perhaps he took out the bed temporarily to make more floor space available—that would not have surprised me. It must be remembered that Mick was at least fifteen years older than the majority of the students and so his behaviour was bound to be different regarding the lecturers, of whom many were his peers. Mick never saw them as better than him or in any way superior.

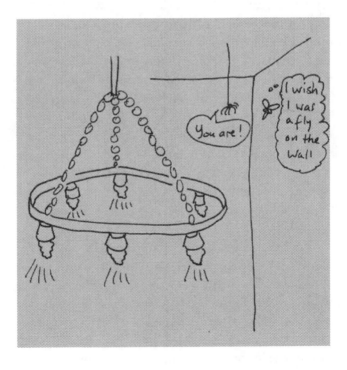

The cleaner, whose task it was to clean the rooms each day, simply couldn't cope with the situation and in the end, after only about eight weeks or so, she came to an arrangement with Mick in that she would not even bother trying to clean his room until he left the following summer. This suited Mick because he didn't give a single thought to tidiness; in fact tidiness irritated him—he thought it such a waste of time. Also, he was totally committed to eccentricity as a way of life even if he didn't admit it as such. Often he would speak of people of his own age with much scorn and denounce and decry their stagnation and boring lives. He thought that somehow he was fighting off the effects of ageing because he rode a bicycle; he was an early eco-militant. He was very interesting to talk to as he mixed up many 'good' ideas with his own nonsense and self-interest. Mick soon became very unpopular with virtually all his lecturers and it was really all his own fault. During his stay at the college every one of Mick's lecturers turned against him except for his Education lecturer, who taught us both. Our Education lecturer was a wonderful man. He had a sense of humour and his patience and understanding of the problems at hand i.e. Mick, seemed to be limitless.

Mick took two main subjects—art and biology. Unfortunately, Mick's behaviour soon caused him to fall out with his first art lecturer. As a result of this Mick was coerced into moving into another group, which in fact was rated much lower than the one from which he was ousted. Mick had talked himself into the top group despite his lack of artistic skill or experience. He was seen as a mature student and therefore more likely to settle down and produce appropriate work. Unpredictably for the art department, Mick's work was of such a high standard that it soon became obvious that they were discriminating against him and, rather than wait for him to kick up one hell of a fuss, they decided to take him back into the main stream again. The lecturer refused to have him back so he was put into the parallel taught by a female lecturer. At first she was really enthralled at having Mick in her group and, under her inspiration and guidance, he started producing really high quality work. Mick blossomed and his new lecturer thought the world of him.

It wasn't to be though. This honeymoon period lasted a few months. She took a fancy to him; but Mick didn't really fancy her at all—with his usual diplomatic grace he told her so in the middle of a lecture—in front of all the other students. She became his most bitter enemy and tried to do two things. She succeeded in her first ploy of getting him thrown out of her group but failed at her second scheme; she was unable to get him thrown out of college. There were two other fine art lecturers left, but they were forewarned and both refused to let Mick join their groups. There was only one other lecturer that he had not offended but this was in the pottery department. Mick had never done any pottery at all and the lecturers probably thought they had got him that time. They expected Mick to fail and they would be able to get rid of him for underachieving. They thought he'd be out of their hair in no time at all.

It backfired on them though; he was a natural with clay and soon, in a matter of weeks, he was making incredible pieces that far excelled all the other students and even the lecturer. At first the lecturer was delighted with the situation and boasted openly of his 'discovery' of Mick. Of course, this didn't last long because Mick shot himself in the foot and did something that once again put him out in the cold. Mick didn't tell me what he had done but, whatever it was, it was enough to bring the guillotine down upon him. He was now banned from all the art lectures and art rooms during the normal day time sessions. For the last eighteen months (half of his college life) he was only allowed to do art after about six o'clock at night until he was ejected by the groundsmen who came to lock up. Everyone in the art department snubbed him and he became a solitary worker—no one could stand being near him because he always ended up causing trouble of one sort or another. He made no friends amongst the student body—they were all suspicious of him; they were wise to be wary.

As time went on the situation became even more tangled and bitter and for the last year Mick was not even allowed to fire any of his pottery in the college. He had to go to another college and pretend there was problem with the kiln at our college. The alternative college let him fire his pots and then sent the bill to him. He passed this on to the Bursar of our college and it caused uproar. The Principal, though she now detested Mick, was shocked to discover that the art department refused to handle his work. She made them give Mick proper facilities for getting his work done. It caused a great deal of anger and animosity of which Mick was totally indifferent to. His skin was tougher than that of a Chieftain tank.

About half of Mick's work in the art department seemed to be made to get at the Christian Union students, who had the college wrapped up in their reactionary grip. The Christian Union group was the only organised group in college and its insidious ideas dominated all aspects of the college. With this group in mind, Mick made a clay fruit bowl containing a huge 'bunch of grapes'. It was shaded a curious and peculiar blue which tended to make it a very confusing object to look at. When I first saw it I thought it rather odd because it had meandering lines running along all the grapes—the lines looked like veins on the back of an old person's hands. I asked what they were and Mick said that, as far as the Christians were concerned, it was simply a bunch of grapes. I told him that I also thought it was grapes but the veins made them look odd. I told him I thought there was something I was missing. He laughed and told me that the grapes weren't grapes at all. The fruit bowl actually contained an enormous bunch of swollen testicles. This was very amusing because all the Christian girls who saw it were enthralled by Mick's craftsmanship and artistry. It was obvious that Mick got a great kick out of letting them look at it, appreciate it, whilst at the same time being wildly mislead.

One of his paintings depicted two lovers in bed. They were both sitting up holding each other tenderly and the whole thing looked schmaltzy and overly sentimental. I thought it rather poor and told Mick it wasn't one of his better pieces of work. Once again I had overlooked something hidden in his work. He told me I'd missed the point completely. He told me to have a close look at the lovers; to look closely below their waistlines. I did as he suggested and at first saw nothing at all; then the penny dropped. I saw that both the lovers, male and female, had penises. He had carefully camouflaged the phalluses and when he pointed them out the obscenity was crystal clear but, to the uninformed, they didn't exist. Once again, Mick had created a work of 'art' whose intention was to ridicule the observer. This deception wasn't an obsession but Mick seemed to get pleasure from misleading his fellow artists. I didn't think this was a very positive trait.

Other objects of Mick's output were less obviously shocking (they probably were but perhaps he didn't let on his innermost thoughts to me). One of them was an unglazed cuboid measuring six inches by six inches by eighteen inches—like an elongated shoebox. This was finished by having a grasping hand coming from the top and curling to one side. It is very hard to describe it and give it justice but everyone who saw it was greatly impressed by it. Actually it was incredibly delicate and Mick realised that he was unable to transport it anywhere without breaking it—it wouldn't have lasted five minutes on his rickety bike. He thus donated it to the art department—this was a great move. He had given them his very best piece of work despite their harassment and obstruction and there was a great deal of embarrassing apologies from the lecturers. He was in his element because he pretended not to even know that they had obstructed him. This made them squirm even more. It was horrible or lovely depending on which side you were.

At the very end of our course we were asked to present work we'd done in our various subjects. The art department had two rooms available for the students to set out their work. Come the day of the exhibition, they had to have three rooms because Mick had produced so much work that he needed a room to himself so as to be able to display everything properly. The exhibition was opened to the general body of students and the public at large and it soon became obvious that everyone was migrating to Mick's 'room' to see his work. It was a fight to get in. The other two rooms were given cursory looks but the main attention went to Mick's work. His exhibition was incredible and included pieces that people could touch and play with. Several dealers had come to pay the usual college visit. They thronged round Mick making bids for his work—he wasn't interested in the slightest in what they were saying. He was quite interested in one offer to work in a pottery in Cornwall but turned it down because he really was only interested in teaching.

Mick was a natural artist. He developed his skills over a four or five year period. The wall paintings he started just before college had been his first attempts at creating something; less than half a decade later he had become extremely talented across a wide range of artistic disciplines. Despite his obvious talent he had next to no knowledge of art and I probably knew more about famous painters than he did. It didn't matter; he didn't know about it but he could do it. What talent!

One of his exhibits was a smoking woman, made entirely from scrap metal that he had found lying around on the college site. A pendulum swung inside the hollow torso which raised and lowered a spindly arm. At the end of the arm was an old, ripped, rubber glove holding a 'spark plug' cigarette. The tip had been painted with bright red nail varnish to imitate a lit end. It was a great favourite with the people coming in to see the exhibition. It may have been inspired by a work by Picasso, but knowing Mick, it was probably inspired by someone he'd met in a newsagent. After a couple of hours a 'guard' was organised by the art department to make sure that no-one stole any of the 'acclaimed' works. Mick didn't give a damn and really couldn't have cared less about it. His motto was 'well if they nick it they must really want it!' I suppose that mirrored his own philosophy about 'borrowing' things he wanted.

Of course all this praise caused divisions among the other art students—they had behaved themselves and conducted their studies in the appropriate manner. Mick has been anarchic; but perhaps he was the truer artist as a result of his rebellious attitude. Although none of the art students had socialised with Mick, they recognised his talent. About half were delighted with his success but a significant number; mainly the Christian contingent, were very hostile and jealous and, of course, they disliked Mick on a personal level anyway. The Principal paid her usual visit to these little 'bye-bye' affairs and was very embarrassed at discovering Mick's success. Several local dignitaries, such as the Mayor, talked enthusiastically about Mick's work and suggested it must be very rewarding having someone as good as him at the college. The Principal felt duty bound to introduce Mick to these people. The Principal was forced to agree that Mick had done a great deal for the college. She must have been biting her tongue off as she was mouthing words, just to keep face.

The Principal had not turned against Mick because of his behaviour in the art department. Her reasons for falling out with him were for something entirely different. During the first and second years there was a drug scare—several students were 'busted' by the college staff but it was all hushed up and dealt with internally. Several of the people busted were friends of Mick and me and so naturally suspicion fell onto the two of us. I lived outside college, in my own bedsit, and that made it rather difficult for the college authorities to do anything about me. I stood out like a sore-thumb with my long hair but I was one of the very few students who didn't smoke cannabis. Mick was also suspected and, since he did live in college he was open to searches. There were two rounds of searches. The first was carried out amid great publicity by a couple of lecturers and Christian Union students. They diligently searched Mick's room and he had a great time because they spent ages looking through his mass of stuff. Mick and I sat there watching. We had refused to leave because Mick didn't want them planting anything. I was to be his witness in case they tried anything.

Of course, they found nothing. I thought they would because I knew for certain that he had some pot somewhere. He'd been smoking some the previous night and I knew he hadn't used it all up. The searchers left empty handed and somewhat disappointed—they knew he had it somewhere. He didn't tell me where he'd put it, which was rather sensible I suppose.

A couple of days later there was another raid. The college authorities thought a surprise raid would catch Mick unawares. Several searchers entered the room without knocking and Mick leapt at them and I thought he was going to smash them down—but Mick wasn't a violent man. I never witnessed anything violence like that of his father. Mick used rude words instead. They hadn't expected him to act like that—they expected him to mildly sit back and allow them to invade his space. His angry response to their entry forced a change of tactics. They apologised for their abrupt entrance but still demanded to search the place. Once again we watched them taking the place apart. One of them worked his way along the bookshelf and started looking at the book of perversions. He studied it rather a long time until Mick asked him if he had found any interesting positions. The Christian Union guy was totally embarrassed and left soon after because he couldn't stand the continual taunts about his funny interests. They found nothing and were forced to concede the fact that Mick was clean. They left rather despondently because they knew Mick had some stuff but they just couldn't prove it.

No sooner were they out the door than Mick sat down and took his shoes off. I hadn't prepared myself for this; I fully expected the smell from his unwashed feet to overwhelm my nostrils and knock me out. I didn't have time to worry about stink feet. Mick surprised me because he stuffed his hands in each shoe and produced two small plastic bags. Each bag had a quantity of dope. He rolled a joint jubilantly, and a few seconds was drifting off into a drug-induced victory celebration.

The Principal was beside herself with worry about the dreadful effects drug taking would have on her 'wards'. She decided to call a meeting of all those students she knew were involved in the affair—not to punish them but to rectify what she thought was a nasty situation and get them back onto the road of their salvation. Before this took place she called Mick to her study and asked him confidentially if he was involved. Mick was horrified and demanded an immediate apology from her for the smear upon his character. She apologised and said that she should have known better than to have even believed Mick was involved. Mick left in triumph.

A couple of days later Mick and I were in a friend's room with several other students and most of them were happily puffing away on the old weed when a Christian Union chap came in. He smelled the pungent, overly sweet air and immediately knew what was happening—it always amazed me that these moral folk always know what cannabis smells like—does the nasal response come with a bible at birth? He left in a rush and reported the discovery but once again nothing could be proved. The Principal decided enough was enough and decided to act; a meeting was to be held one evening in a common room in the main block. I didn't go since I had never taken the stuff and, to be honest, I found the 'drug—scene' boring and, being a non-smoker, I found it horribly smelly. I never enjoyed sitting in rooms with people puffing away on the silly stuff.

A large number of people decided to attend the meeting having heard the call from on high. Another 'unofficial' message was also sent out along the grapevine that 'everybody' who was involved had to attend and Mick, despite his earlier meeting with the Principal, thought he should go along to hear her speaking. The room was packed solid with about fifty students. The Principal was horrified at such a large turnout and was, for a few moments, unable to speak to them. She had to gather her thoughts together as she surveyed the room. She was particularly annoyed to see Mick there; she never trusted him again. She spoke to them all about the 'problem'. No one really paid much attention to the college authorities and the Christian Union purges, and the whole thing collapsed when the Christian Union was itself investigated and many leading members were themselves discovered to be smoking dope. This public debacle hardly dented the authority of the Christian Union though. They had the place tied up.

Mick became very hostile to the Principal and wanted to get his own back on her. He decided he would produce a college magazine with the sole intention of writing horrible things about her. The editorial board of the proposed publication would have two members—me and Mick. He was going to make everything up and try to cause a scandal to get her sacked. I had not seen this horrible side of him before and it was very much out of character; he did weird stuff but he didn't usually do things to hurt anyone. He chatted with me several times about how we should proceed. I took it upon myself to talk him out of it. He had no idea of the mechanics of collating and printing so he was starting from rock bottom. I knew the mechanics of printing, and had access to such devices through my political connections, but I had no intention of sharing those resources with Mick on his harebrained scheme. I pointed out the numerous problems and it was fairly easy to derail his mission. I was relieved when this little scheme disappeared off the radar. We were able to get back to our normal state of non-malevolent chaos.

Despite the fact that Mick did exceptionally well in art it wasn't his main subject of study—biology was. He was in the same group as me and I can clearly remember the first time I ever went to a lecture with him. It was when I first started at the college. Mick took me in and took much pleasure in introducing me to everyone in the group. The lecturer eyed me cautiously and then turned to Mick and asked if he was playing a prank on them. They were so used to his eccentric behaviour that they thought I was simply someone from outside college trying to get a higher education for free. They wouldn't accept his word and rang through on the internal telephone to check up with the main office. My status was confirmed and I was welcomed into the group. It seemed that my enrolment was a positive move because my arrival meant there was an equal number of males and females. At last, the imbalance of the small group would be rectified. My start seemed to be most optimistic but it didn't work out quite as positively as the lecturers hoped.

The biology group was a curious assembly of odd-bods. They varied from the Christian Union women to a fascist, eastern European megalomaniac. My time in that group with Mick was a continual battle between the males. Incessant quarrelling and argument destroyed every lecture and practical session. The females were all lightweight Christian Union members and always the very 'best' students; they behaved properly and worked hard. We males, on the other hand, were awful. The foul-foursome consisted of me, Mick, the eastern European named Jacob and Simon, an ex-public school boy.

Simon was hopelessly out of his depth throughout the whole course and his lack of background knowledge and lack of ability put him at a continual disadvantage; he just didn't seem to understand things very easily. It was made much worse for him because he had to work alongside a bunch of anarchists—i.e. the rest of us. Simon had an additional problem; because he had attended a public school he thought himself superior to the rest of us. That didn't go down at all well and we rarely helped him out. In fact, we did our best to needle him at every opportunity. Simon always fell in to whatever trap we set for him. We took great delight in sabotaging his experiments; we would switch chemicals or dilute them to make them ineffective. Whilst the rest of us produced results, of sorts, he would watch his experiments as nothing happened. It was all very childish but so addictive. His pomposity set him up for attack—and he certainly got it.

Jacob was a constant thorn in my side because he was always going on about General Sikorski—the eastern European War leader who was knocked off by Churchill (or so I was given the impression). I was constantly arguing with Jacob about his fascist beliefs and activities—he was all for 'strong' government and spoke at great length about how he would liquidate the 'commies' and the unions. I am confident that he would have lined me up against a wall and filled me full of lead given half a chance. Although we were at loggerheads and Jacob would have gunned me down if the chance arose we actually got on rather well. He even invited me back to his home and his Mum, who spoke no English, cooked us a meal. It went really well. After the meal we chatted for a while and I discovered that Jacob played the piano. We had a good time. Jacob could play 'by ear' and he was able to play any tune I suggested. This little event made things better between us but even so, once we were back in college, we settled back into our argumentative ways. We were impossible.

If Jacob and I were bad, then the four of us together were even worse; we made a riotous team. The sum of the males was much worse than the parts. The females, on the other hand, always achieved the desired results whenever they undertook experimental work simply because they co-operated with each other; they discussed things, they shared results and made constructive criticisms of results. We males did not have one successful experiment in the whole three years; we constantly bickered amongst ourselves about how best to run the experiment, or how to read data, or how to draw conclusions and so on—it was tedious.

If there was a simple operation such as weighing a flask we would each get wildly different measurements and refuse to believe we were wrong. Every experiment we wrote up contained long passages on the 'factors' that caused the erroneous results. Of course, there was a common thread running through our failure. We were the common factor and, in desperation, the senior biology lecturer demanded that the group worked as two teams each containing two members of either gender. I was put in the same team as Jacob and, of course, we argued all the time and eventually ended up by ruining the females' work as well. Mick was in the other group with Simon and their disagreements ruined that group too. It was a total disaster and the lecturer called us all together and told us we were totally useless and threatened all manner of sanctions. She even had cross words with the females who had been lambs for the slaughter—oh well, at least it followed in the Christian tradition. The lecturer's words had no impact; they went in one ear and out the other. She needed a way of pinning us down and she managed to get our attention. She suggested we would not be able to go on field trips. Finally, we were all listening attentively. At last, she had found something that hit home. This calmed us down and we listened to what she was saying. We were like the Fenn Street Gang from Please Sir—but we were no longer school kids; we just behaved that way.

The field trips were held in the south west of England and we'd heard from other students that they were very enjoyable. For me it was a delight to go back; the time with Mick had been a great experience. We looked forward to the trip so we played ball for a while and our collaboration in the laboratories may have even been partially successful. The lecturer appreciated the calmer atmosphere and we managed to complete assignments. The lecturer was shocked when we volunteered to help with the packing and preparation for the trip. The four males manhandled all the scientific equipment down the four flights of stairs and helped pack them into the coach. We did it all without any squabbling; had we rehabilitated ourselves? We were creating such a good impression.

The coach was rather dilapidated and looked like a vehicle from one of the early St Trinian films. We set off on a Saturday morning in a very positive mood. There was much jollity and we even sang songs together. The trip was going well although the driver seemed to be over-revving the engine. We ignored this and continued to enjoy ourselves. Our enjoyment was interrupted when the coach driver made an unexpected stop along a main road. He managed to park partially on the grass verge but even so there was soon a long tailback of vehicles trying to pass us. The driver told us there was a problem with the accelerator cable; it seemed to be sticking. He told us he'd have to walk back to the town we had passed through and find a telephone box to call for a repair vehicle. It seemed we might be unable to get to our destination after all. Simon surprised us all. He said he knew something about coaches because his dad owned a company and had shown him how they worked. We were somewhat sceptical of his talent but he set forth purposefully and within minutes he had raised a couple of floor panels exposing the road beneath. He peered down into the mechanical pits and quickly identified the problem. A bracket had snapped and the cable was snagging. Simon used some string to jury-rig a repair. We were most impressed at his skilful resolution to the problem. It was the first time he had ever done anything positive or for the benefit of others. Naturally we reacted to this human act. Jacob and I decided we'd reward him somehow when we got to the hotel. Jacob came up with the idea himself.

We arrived a little later than expected and we drove into the car park of a hotel just at the outskirts of the town; it was a very steep climb up the hill. The hotel was pleasant enough. Jacob and I began our reward for Simon's unselfish act on the coach. We told him the rotas for room sharing had already been prepared but there was one problem; one pair of males would have to share a room. Mick and Simon had been teamed together for this—it was not fair but two of us had to share. Jacob embellished the sharing story with a small twist. He told Simon that he had to share a double bed with Mick. Simon went as white as a sheet and said he refused, point blank, and would leave for home if that was really the situation he faced. We continued egging him on and he went off to complain to the lecturers about the situation. We headed him off just before he confronted them and put him out of his misery—he was incredibly relieved to see his own individual sleeping arrangements. Although he didn't have to share the same bed he did have to share the same room. Despite being Mick's best friend I had quickly got out of sharing with him because I knew I could expect peculiar things to happen. I chose Jacob even though we were sparring with each other all the time. I knew I would have an easier time with him than I would with Mick. After Simon's help on the coach our game was a bit harsh but Simon had been such a pain for months; we couldn't resist the prank.

The hotel didn't know what had hit it. We were unlike any other group of students that had stayed there previously. The hotel was used previous parties from our college fitting in and behaving sensibly. After a couple of days of trying to cope with us the hotel management decided they had to isolate us from the other guests. We were served our meals after all the other guests had finished. This was for two reasons. Firstly, we were so incredibly noisy and secondly, Mick's table manners were those of a pig. I was used to his snatching and grabbing and gobbling at the table; I knew that his chewing with his mouth open wasn't due to choking. He made a noise like splattering mud as he chomped his mouth up and down. The hotel staff contacted our lecturers who in turn came to me to ask if there was anything to be done about Mick. They really thought I had some control over him; they were way off target on that one. I explained the situation about his lack of manners and the only viable option for the hotel was to suggest that our party ate after the other guests. I suppose they could have put a box over his head but it would have been rather unfriendly. I believe it was so serious that the management had threatened to ask us to leave. A compromise had to be found otherwise we would have been evicted and forced to return to college early. The knock-on effects for the lecturers would have been awful. The isolation worked, on the whole, and peace returned to the hotel.

A few days after we arrived we were strolling along eastwards along the beach when Mick came upon two teenage boys fishing. He went over to them and started chatting about what they had caught. They had not had much luck. I hoped Mick would leave them alone but he carried on the conversation well beyond the bounds of normal convention. I became very concerned because he wasn't just chatting to them; I got the impression he was trying his luck. I kept interrupting with comments about our work and attempting to get him to leave them alone. I couldn't help but feel uncomfortable being with him as he wormed his way into their confidence. Mick ignored me and he wouldn't move until he had learnt everything about them. It worked out that they were on a camping trip but weren't having much success with their tent; they were trying to catch their dinner but had no luck with that either. It brought back memories of my own experience of Mick, with the two fish, a few summers earlier. Mick listened and as they talked he worked out a cunning scheme to help them.

The solution was obvious; at least it was to him. Mick calmly invited them back to the hotel to stay in his room. I was horrified—I fully expected him to do something silly but I was appalled at the thought of the two youngsters staying in his room. I wasn't party to the arrangements that were worked out between them but I knew something was afoot. I warned Simon to expect visitors at some point but had no other information. The two lads came to the hotel after dark. They crept across the car park with all their gear and fishing tackle and crept into Mick's room, which was conveniently on the ground floor and had bay windows. Once inside they showed Mick their day's catch—after we'd left them they had managed to catch a few fish. Since they were hungry, Mick suggested they cook the fish, in the room, on the primus stove they had with them. Very soon the smell of fish was wafting from his room; you can't hide the smell of fish when you're cooking. Since the room faced the car park most of the fishy smell escaped through the open doorway into the car park. The open door allowed most of the pong to drift out into the night but not all the smell escaped. The smell filtered under and around the door into the hall and then proceeded to permeate its way through the whole hotel. There was a noticeable fish pong pervading the corridors. The hotel staff tried to track down the cause of the smell but couldn't find it. They knew it was coming from the block we were in but couldn't identify the room. Fortunately, the smell died away once the fish was eaten and cleared away. Each room had a basin so the dishes and pan had all traces of the fish washed away.

The hotel cleaners were confused by the smell the next day as they cleaned Mick's room. Mick said he'd brought some samples back from the beach and they had gone off. Sensing a rat, the cleaners were very suspicious but, since we had so much gear in the room and also we were a 'Biology' group, they had to accept his word. By now we had acquired a reputation of being that 'odd lot' from London. The two lads stayed all week and we stole food for them from the kitchens—I thought it better to provide them with food rather than have the hassle of more complaints about odd smells. Mick kept everything platonic with the boys and they left without incident. Was he losing his touch? Why had he not made a move on them? I was quite surprised by Simon; I had expected him to raise hell about the invasion of the lads into the room and complain about the cramped conditions. He reacted completely differently; he thought the whole thing was a great wheeze and thoroughly enjoyed the game he was wrapped up in. He provided more food for them than the rest of us put together; he was showing a completely different side to himself.

On the very first day of the trip we walked into a meadow just outside the town. The purpose was to try to identify and classify as many species of plants as we could. Our lecturer started us off by pointing out a few specimens but after only one or two examples she was interrupted by Mick, who said she'd given us the wrong name for one of the plants. The lecturer was understandably angered by his interruption and told Mick he was wrong—he should be quiet and listen. Oops! This was a rag to a bull. I knew something would happen. Mick interrupted her again by giving us all a quick lecture on the plant in question starting with the Latin name and genus and so on. The lecturer had mis-identified a species of vetch. I didn't know a vetch from my elbow and neither did any of the other students. Mick knew the names of all the vetch plants that were native to the British Isles.

The lecturer stopped arguing with him and confidently picked up a 'Collins' guide to prove him wrong and put him in his place. She was determined to show her authority. Oops! She didn't know about Mick's encyclopaedic knowledge of plants. She was proved wrong and Mick was totally vindicated. Undaunted, she carried on giving us her guided tour until once again she was interrupted by Mick. This time she simply said 'Okay if you know so much, do it yourself'. Mick did. He took over and, with great enthusiasm, led us through the meadow and named every plant pointed out to him. The number of plants growing in a field is incredible, and the species count massive, and yet Mick knew them all. His only problem was identifying certain types of grasses but after a single glance at the photographs of the various types he had no problem. His knowledge of botany was simply phenomenal and he put the lecturer to great shame for which she never forgave him (understandably). For the rest of us it was a game as we spotted new plants and asked Mick for identification. He barely hesitated before giving a confident reply. He knew the common names as well as the Latin names; he also knew the habitats and key features of the plants. He really knew his stuff.

As part of the course we had to perform an experiment with molasses. We spread this onto trees and, because of its sticky texture; it trapped any insects and other small creatures that attempted to feed on it. When we came to painting the trees with the molasses we noticed that it was incredibly runny. It should have had the consistency of thick honey but it was much closer to water. We discussed it and agreed that it must be a new type that became thicker after contact with the air. Maybe it went semi-solid as it dried in the air. We painted our targeted tree trunks and left the molasses to do what we expected. We returned the next morning to see the fruits of our labour and identify which species of insects we had trapped. We were expecting a large crop of insects, beetles, moths and maybe a few butterflies. There were none. We had caught nothing at all. The molasses had completely disappeared leaving no more than a light stain on the trees. We didn't find any insect bodies at all but there were lots of well-fed insects in the wood that day. We had no more molasses and also we had run out of time so we were unable to repeat the experiment, it had to be abandoned. That night, Mick confessed to me that he had sabotaged the experiment. When he learnt what was intended he decided to intervene to prevent the murder of the innocent animals. He took the molasses from the room where all our equipment was stored and he had diluted it to make it runny and ineffective. His intention to stop the experiment had worked; no animals were harmed in the painting of the molasses.

Every evening, after we had finished writing up the notes of the day, we all walked the half mile or so down into the town. We took along a plastic, half-gallon container which we had filled with 'scrumpy' cider in one of the local pubs.

Having filled our container we headed down to the sea front and sat there getting drunk. Even the Christian Union girls came along though they drank in moderation, of course. Even so, it tended to round off the day quite well and made us friendlier towards each other. It was really relaxing sitting on the beach, looking out to sea, and drinking the potent liquid. We were enjoying each other's company and the squabbling was put on hold for a short time. When we got back to college we were at each other's throats again, though.

On the last night, we were in one of the hotel reception rooms. It was well after one o'clock in the morning and Mick decided to give us all a tune on the piano. It was all very amusing because he couldn't play. He banged any key he felt like and sang along. He sounded as bad as you could imagine. After a couple of minutes we'd had enough and walked out. He finished immediately and went to bed as well. In the morning Jacob was called into the office of the hotel and taken to task for playing the piano at such a late hour. He was told that there had been numerous complaints about the noise. Jacob said he hadn't done it, but since he was the only one of us known to be able to play the piano, he got the blame. Having been balled out by the hotel staff he was given a going over by the lecturers who threatened all sorts of things once we were back at college. It was all very amusing; they couldn't even tell the difference between his 'playing' and Mick's 'music'. Actually Jacob played quite well except that he made every tune sound like a military march. He could play by ear but it always came out with the drama of the Dam Busters theme tune. Of course he was really angry about copping it for something he hadn't done (he wasn't even in the room which made it so much harder for him to stomach) but since the rest of us were united against him he had to lump it—he sulked all the way back to London.

Those early days were chaotic; I lived outside college and would arrive about twenty minutes before the first lecture that started at 9:15 a.m. I would immediately make my way up to Mick's room, knock on his door and wake him up. He was never awake. I would knock again on his door and then enter because I knew he wouldn't acknowledge my presence otherwise. Once I was in the room he would slowly get out of bed. He didn't wear pyjamas but chose instead to wear his vest and underpants which, due to constant use, were a lovely shade of grey. He would pull on his shirt from the previous day and then slip his tie over his head and loop it around his neck. His tie was always left in a loop so as to be able to be slipped over his neck and fastened in a matter of seconds. Invariably one collar was sticking up at an odd angle. He'd then make a quick pot of tea (in the solid silver pot naturally) and a few slices of toast. Whilst the kettle was boiling and the toast was browning he'd wander off to the toilet down the hall to do what was necessary. He'd come back and make the tea. He'd pour it into stained cracked cups that had seen better days. The toast was covered with butter in his smear method. Whilst drinking and eating he'd pull on his trousers and corduroy jacket and a pair of shoes and then be ready for the day. He looked like an untidy version of Patrick Moore—unbelievable but true. Once, he wore a pair of odd shoes; I didn't say a word to him as he slipped them on. I had great fun telling him about his mistake halfway through a lecture. He looked down and noticed his error. I thought he wouldn't be bothered but I got it very wrong. He was really embarrassed and curled his legs under his chair. It looked as though he was trying to stick one leg up the other trouser leg. He writhed on his chair throughout the lecture and that made it even worse because he simply drew attention to himself until everyone knew his plight.

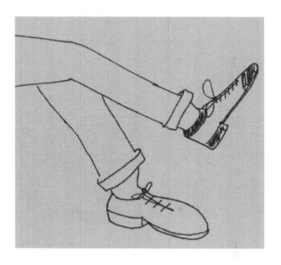

We had to attend PE sessions as part of our course and Mick really didn't feel at home with these sessions. On one occasion we had to go in to a gym to be shown some basic PE techniques to use with young school children. We were told to sit in a circle whilst two or three students climbed ropes that reached up to the ceiling; we were expected to shout out encouraging words to help them make their ascent. My turn came around and I surprised everyone by being so nimble; I was really good at it. I had always been good at climbing so I found climbing a thick rope no problem at all. I was amongst the best at carrying out this activity. Mick's turn came around—he was hopeless and there was a noticeable level of sniggering at his predicament. Mick had the last laugh though. He persisted and managed to drag himself upwards until he finally reached about two thirds of the way up. As he made his way upwards his legs would swing about in a most ungainly fashion but there was worse to come. He was wearing baggy shorts without underpants and, as he swung back and forward, his courting tackle was displayed to all watching from below. It was not a pleasant sight. The laughing stopped. Mick's public display had certainly got their full attention. Mick didn't make it all the way up and slid back to the floor. He then joined me where I was sitting. He sat with his legs crossed in front of him so that nearly everyone had a full view of his manhood. He did it deliberately; there were many discomforted students sitting in front of him.

As time went on Mick lost the support of the Biology lecturers as well as those in the art department. The position he found himself in was of his own making. He had developed an approach to living things, which bordered on fanaticism. He thought all living things had a soul—it was as bad killing an ant as it was killing a person. Actually, Mick thought killing people was a lesser evil. One of our pieces of experimental work was based on an investigation of different types of the drosophila fruit fly. We had to breed the tiny insects in large glass bell jars because we needed populations in the hundred thousands from which to take random samples. These fly bred like—well, they bred like flies. The bottom of each container was a layer of food in gel form. We added new gel every day to allow the bulging population to feed itself. The flies bred so quickly that the jars soon became black with them. Carefully, we would knock them out with a tiny amount of chloroform and select a few individuals at random. After checking them they were replaced to keep the experiment valid. We were checking characteristics such as eye colour and size of wings. These observations were to help us understand the mechanics of genetics in action.

When we had finished the experiment Mick asked what was going to happen to the billions of flies in his container (we all had our own bell jars full of the little critters). When told they were going to be killed by chloroform Mick went mad. He grabbed his jar from out of the hands of the lecturer and called her a murderer. He ran from the room and down the six flights of stairs until he was on the ground floor. He opened the door and made his way outside. We were watching from the windows above and saw him standing on the large grass bank outside the building. He opened his jar and let the flies have a taste of freedom and the chance of liberty. It was an empty gesture; they fell, almost as a solid lump, to the ground. They were dead! They hadn't stood a chance because it was mid-winter and the cold had killed them at once. Mick had killed them off much more quickly than did the lecturer. Mick was really upset; he felt like he was the murderer.

Unfortunately, his views on human beings didn't quite match up to his love and affection for animals in general. During one lecture on world population he suddenly interrupted with a theory of his own that he was developing. Basically he felt that the way to solve the human population increase was by knocking down houses and thereby giving people fewer places to breed—he actually said that! He thought 'intelligent' people i.e. himself, should be encouraged to have children but everyone else should have to pass an intelligence test to see if they were worthy. He really detested most people and would have traded them for a daffodil bulb without a qualm.

Things reached rock bottom when he halted one of the lectures to tell the lecturer that she was an evil, wicked woman and she shouldn't be allowed to corrupt our minds. She had been talking about the pros and cons of vivisection and Mick had taken great offence to her words. She had been impartial in her use of words but, as far as Mick was concerned, she was advocating the systematic torture of God's creatures and that should not be allowed to happen. None of us took him that seriously because his ideas were so inconsistent—since he cared so little for his own species we were doubtful whether his commitment to the lower forms of life actually amounted to much more than hot air. This time the lecturer had had enough; she demanded an apology from Mick but this only made him worse and in the end she told him to leave the lecture and not return before he apologised for his behaviour. He said he would gladly go since he could learn more from books anyway. The lecturer refused to have him back in her group and this effectively meant he didn't have lectures in his main subject for half of his final year. I was curious as to how he would learn from books—he didn't read any. Maybe he had x-ray vision.

This ban from attending lectures or using the facilities also coincided with the time when it became necessary for us to hand in our special studies that we'd been working on during the whole of the course. Mick had chosen some highly original work on spiders and after a fantastic amount of research he'd written his discoveries and observations up in a hard backed notebook. Mick modelled his book upon the style used by early naturalists. He went to great pains to make his work neat and his diagrams were simply superb and were so good that the Biology department refused to believe he had actually done it himself. The work was of such a high standard that they refused to accept it and made him do another one from scratch. Mick did another study, in less than a month, and this he simply made up. He claimed to have discovered a new species of spider—not an implausible suggestion as there are so many 'undiscovered' ones out there awaiting classification. Mick wrote up the mating habits of this fictional arachnid and handed it in. They accepted it and he passed the assessment. In this same month he also wrote another study for Simon. Simon had been prevaricating about what he should do for nearly three years. He hadn't even started when the time came around for handing them in came. He was in a mad panic and in desperation he asked Mick for his help. Mick surprised me and agreed. He and Simon slept out in a local wood for several nights in a row and studied the moths that were attracted to a torch light. Mick wrote the results up and this was enough for our weasely associate to pass. Most of this 'study' was as fictitious as Mick's own study on spiders.

Mick carried on his biological studies despite the ban. He enrolled me in his alternative approach. Every so often he would ask me to 'borrow' items from the lab and I would arrange to do this for him. I tried to return everything after he had used it; he borrowed a rather expensive electronic microscope and I almost got caught when I returned it to its storage cupboard. I mentioned this to one of my friends outside college and this friend became really interested. He asked me if I could get hold of a projector; my friend had some slides that he wanted to display. I checked through the stock room and discovered a large optical device that would act as a projector if part of its mechanism was removed. I took the item home and showed it to my friend. He suggested viewing the slides after we had been for a drink. We went to our local haunt and met up with several other mates and our intended drink became several drinks. When we got back he asked me to set up the imitation projector for the assembled company. It cast a strong image onto the opposite wall. Fortunately, the wall was painted a very pale colour and so the reflection was very good. My friend took out his slides and presented the first one to the beam of light.

The projection was successful. Oh dear! The image on the wall was very explicit indeed. I had never seen a real pornographic image until this point. Now I was in at the deep end. There were several women dressed as school girls and they had an equal number of male partners. Nothing was left to the imagination. Apart from the obscenity of the images there was a small problem. The projection only displayed about a quarter of the slide. I had to jiggle it to show the entire image—as I did so there were cries for me to hurry up. There was an additional problem; if the slide remained in the beam too long it overheated and melted. I am afraid to say that the persons presenting themselves on the slides had all their intimate parts boiled away. My friend wasn't too happy about the destruction of the slides; I wasn't too pleased either—I'd really had my fingers burnt. I took the projector back to college the next day—I didn't really want any repeat performances. My flat mates thought I was a bit of a prude. My girlfriend at the time was a radical feminist and had she known how 'male' I had been she would have turned me to stone—having removed one or two minor appendages first.

In his first year Mick bought a deluxe German tape recorder and this was a very complicated machine. It had a tape inside it that was about sixteen inches across. The tape slowly unwound from a feed spool; the tape was read as it passed a read/write head and then the tape was rewound onto a pick-up spool. The tape was divided into twenty-six tracks which in turn were sub-divided into eight further bands. The tracks started from A1 and went through the alphabet until Z8. Each individual track lasted twenty-five minutes or more and by automatic settings the machine could work through from track A1 to Z8 continuously.

This was about one hundred hours of listening time. There was only one recording and reading head so, as each track of the tape ended, the tape had to be rewound and the head moved onto the adjacent tack. This could have sounded odd but, because the machine was of German construction, the change sounded efficient. A dial on the front allowed the user to determine which track was to be started. Eight push buttons then allowed individual sub-tracks to be selected. Although the machine was only mono it still had very good sound reproduction—it was much better than anything I had heard previously.

Mick bought this machine so that he could read his 'one' book into it and play it back to himself whilst sleeping. Someone had told him that listening to words in your sleep helped you learn them. His reading voice was wonderfully soporific and would be a great purchase for any sufferers of insomnia; they could listen to him at night and soon they'd be cured of all their sleeping problems. He'd soon have them yawning and bored into blissful sleep. For about three months he played it whenever he was sleeping in his room. Had it been a useful book it would probably have done him some good but, unfortunately, it was well out of date and therefore he was learning misleading information all the time. Actually he didn't seem to learn much at all from it and ended up being more confused than enlightened. One day he told me that he'd put the machine to good use; he'd invited a woman up to his room and after getting her high on dope he'd had his way with her, all the time his reading boomed out over the two of them. I suppose it was the ultimate turn on for him to hear himself in the background.

Having introduced the fact that Mick slept with women, I'd better clear up his sexuality. It was simple—he was bisexual. If he took a fancy to anyone the gender was irrelevant. In many ways this seems a much more optimistic proposition as he had twice the number of people to choose from (except that his 'peculiar' normal behaviour would put so many off). Several women in the college were attracted by his 'strangeness' and he had them and ate them up like hot dinners. As soon as he knew someone was interested in him he pounced. Mick didn't seem very interested in long term relationships. Once he had satisfied his loins he dropped his conquests as soon as he could—this left them confused but none of them resented him for very long; I don't remember any of them holding a grudge. His only bad luck was with the rejection by his art lecturer whom I mentioned earlier. One woman, who wore very black clothes—a pre-Goth, was on his mind for months and he was becoming quite obsessed by her. She had a long-term boyfriend in college and it was common knowledge that the two of them slept together. In 1970, in the college, this was still seen as 'not good form'. They got away with it because she was incredibly bright and could argue the pants off anyone including her lecturers. She certainly argued the pants off Mick—or was it the other way around? Eventually he had his way and not long after, she lost her charm. They were an item for a very short time; Mick was rather indiscreet about what the two of them did together. Whilst it was a brand new conquest he was really interested in her. Her affair with Mick had a knock on affect as it ended her relationship with her boyfriend. He had already dropped out of college and now he was out of her life. She remained moderately friendly with Mick—what did he have that kept them happy after he'd dumped them?

Late in our second year at college he decided to grow a beard. He looked like a throwback to the Dark Ages and I started thinking of him as Wildman—he really did look uncivilised. He looked as weird as the singer 'Wildman Fischer' who, in the years of flower power, wrote such gems as the following:

In the year of 1961
I did it all in fun.
In the year of 1962
I got thrown out of school
In the year of 1963
I was committed to a mental institution

An evening with Wildman Fischer—1968 LP

These words almost seemed right for Mick, though I have no proof he attended an institution—I would not be surprised to learn that he had. His beard added another dimension to his wide range of offensive behaviours. As he sat talking to you, he would constantly stuff the shaggy growth into his mouth and suck it until there were several soggy strands hanging limply around his lips. The beard grew to such monstrous dimensions that Mick was asked to trim it. He was on teaching practice and his headteacher called him in and told him to either cut it or get out of the school. Since Mick really wanted to teach he had no choice but to do as he was told. He snipped off a half inch or so but the headteacher wasn't satisfied and demanded a greater cut. Mick complied by removing another half inch. This satisfied the headteacher fortunately. Later on in his teaching practice, he was again asked to trim his beard but this time; the headteacher backed down rather than have a major incident.

There were several amusing incidents revolving around his teaching practice. We were both placed in schools that meant long travelling and thus a very early start every morning. My living outside of college meant I had to get up at five thirty but this soon became too much and I 'dossed' down on a floor in college so as to be able to lie in till half past six. At a quarter to seven we went in to a very early breakfast. Neither of us had any right to do this because the meal was intended only for students living on the campus. This didn't deter us in the slightest and even though the Christian Union students reported us we still continued to go in. Actually there was nothing worse than eating breakfast with Mick at that time in the morning, but the choice was simple. I either ate then or I didn't eat until mid-day—my stomach overcame my reservations.

At seven thirty we boarded a coach, which took us out to our allotted schools in north London. Mick was in a school with one of the Christian Union leaders who had searched his room for drugs. They rather detested each other and the practice was an unfriendly experience for them both as they had to walk together for about half a mile from their dropping off point. Also, the Christian Union toady immediately got on very well with the head of the school—religion was a key component—and thus had an 'excellent' practice.

Mick had an interesting time. Each day he would get back on the coach with another little tale of his experiences and, when he chose to speak loudly, those sitting near us would listen in disbelief. Some of his stories of his teaching methods are rather amusing, some are outrageous. He taught biology and as soon as he was in the school he looked over all his groups and decided which kids were the leaders and/or troublemakers. These kids he kept behind after each lesson to bribe with cigarettes, sweets and money. They kept control of his classes for him and he never had the same sorts of problems that the rest of us mugs were having. The head of department at the school simply couldn't understand why Mick was so successful. No-one was able to teach these groups and yet Mick had them eating out of the palm of his hand—well, out of the pouches in his wallet. It cost him quite a bit but, since he was only doing it for a matter of weeks, it didn't matter too much—it was simply a sound investment for his future prospects. His bullyboys did admirably.

His other methods of teaching were equally innovative. He used to sing and dance to the kids. They would ask him to sing a particular song and he'd do his best to crucify it. The teacher in charge caught him doing this once and called him out of the room to explain himself. Mick said it was his way of relieving tension and hostility in the classroom—he didn't mention the little fact of bribery and corruption. The teacher had to admit that despite the activity, Mick was doing really well with his groups and so Mick was allowed to carry on his novel 'approach'.

Mick was told that cross-country running was to be put on his timetable from the next day. This was to be a regular weekly event; Mick was included just to ensure that teachers were spread out along the whole length of the race. Mick got on the coach that evening and asked everyone on it if they had a spare pair of shorts. No one had any—at least that's what they claimed. In truth, who in their right mind would run the risk of letting Mick put his crotch inside his or her shorts? No-one was quite that stupid! Consequently, he was in a jam but, ever a resourceful soul, he soon overcame his problem. He had an old pair of corduroy trousers and with two quick snips he had turned them into a pair of makeshift shorts. Although he was a skilled artist his tailoring skills were most inadequate and the shorts looked awful. Mick had not attempted to finish the cuts with a hem—no, the material hung loose showing the erratic line of the scissor cut.

The other student at Mick's school took me to one side when we were waiting for the coach to take us back to college. He told me what had happened the next day. Mick went on the cross-country run as directed but since he was a poor athlete he very quickly got left behind. He staggered along, with the rest of the 'unfits' and arrived back at school, in the middle of break, and had to run the gauntlet of the kids in the playground. His agoraphobia took over and he froze up. The whole playground assembled round him and started screaming 'Hot pants! 'Hot pants!' The teaching staff rushed to the windows of the staff room. They wanted to see the cause of the commotion and were astonished to see the mass of humanity converging around Mick. The headteacher screamed out to all present to 'get that maniac in before there's a riot'. Mick was rescued and funnily enough he was taken off the running. That suited him fine anyway. His fellow student was dreadfully embarrassed by the incident.

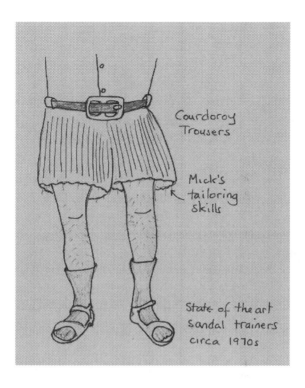

In the laboratory, where Mick taught most of his lessons, he kept a notebook, which he left at the back of the class for the kids to write comments. He saw this as allowing them to say things to him that they'd be scared to say in normal circumstances. This was a very good idea and I was very interested to see what they had written about him. He showed me the book at the end of the practice and there were several really good comments in it. These suggested ways the lessons may have been improved and so on. Also in the book were hundreds of obscene drawings and comments. These ranged from the simple 'fuck offs' to some rather bizarre drawings of Mick's genitalia. Despite its half percent success rate Mick was really pleased with it because he really felt he had helped the kids say things that they needed to say but were normally unable to do. I never quite worked out my feelings on that one. It surprised me that Mick was even interested in what the kids thought about hi. He must have heard about this feedback method in a lecture—it was not likely that he had read about it for reasons disclosed earlier.

Mick did have one spot of trouble from one boy. Every lesson Mick would take a register of those present and one particular boy was repeatedly away. In the end he checked up on the kid and found out that the kid went to every lesson except his. In fact he was never away from school, except for Mick's lessons. Mick collared the kid and got him to attend the lesson. Unfortunately, even though Mick physically took him to the room it still seemed like the kid vanished once he was in the classroom. In the end, Mick tired of trying to find the kid. One day, towards the end of his time in the school, Mick heard a humming. He looked round his group but couldn't see anyone doing it. He traced the noise until he came to one of the small cupboards underneath one of the workbenches. He opened the door and found the miscreant inside reading a comic. The kid was rammed in and in a most uncomfortable position and yet he preferred this to Mick's lessons. There was a moral there somewhere.

On the very last day of the practice the Christian Union toady came up to me and boasted of how he'd been offered a job at the school. He also mentioned the fact that whilst in with the Head, he'd been told that Mick was the most peculiar student they'd ever had the misfortune to have. He gloried in this—I resented it. It may have been totally true but I felt a loyalty to Mick—he was my friend.

I had a problem one morning. I had overslept and had to race in to college to catch the coach. I was so late that I decided to take a short cut and this meant I had to climb over a locked gate. As I slid over the obstacle I felt the back of my trousers catch on something. As I dropped down I heard the tell-tale sign of my trousers ripping. I had torn the backside out of them. I had no choice but carry on and get on the coach. I asked if anyone had a needle and cotton but no-one was able to help me. I arrived at the school dreading the day that was to unfold. I slipped into the staffroom and told my predicament to the teachers I knew. I was really lucky; after the initial roar of laughter, one of the women—she was in her early thirties and had a soft spot for me—took me off to her room. She let me use her stockroom where, with needle and thread that she lent me, I was able to repair the damage. I didn't do a particularly good job on my trousers but no one noticed. I even went for a drink at lunchtime and bought my 'friend' a drink to say thank you. There are always kind people waiting to help. I rather fancied the woman was she was at least ten years my senior and I was far too shy to have suggested anything.

Towards the end of his first year Mick adopted two young American lads that he had discovered on one of his little wanderings. The two chaps were my age and had travelled across to England to escape the draft. Had they stayed in the States they would have been shipped off to Vietnam and in 1970 this was becoming increasingly unpopular and very life threatening. The prospect of being returned home in a black body-bag did not appeal to either of them. They were a couple of really nice lads who were really suffering the loss of their country. They were so proud to be Americans and yet they loathed the war and all America was doing. Mick allowed them to stay in his room with him for a couple of months until they managed to find something more suitable. It was a surprising act of kindness. Mick was able to feed them because he took extra food from the dining hall and would arrive back in his room with enough supplies to keep them going.

The college had halls that were given over to act as dining rooms for breakfast, lunch and evening dinner. I was living outside college so I had no right to use the facilities. Mick thought I was being ridiculous so he invited me in to the meals as his guest. For several months I was able to eat heartily despite the fact that I shouldn't have done so. No-one noticed and there was no checking going on so unless I made myself stand out in some way there would not be a problem.

Mick helped me stand out. The other students would tend to sit together and arrange for a couple of students to arrive early and reserve seats. Mick and I, in our usual laid-back fashion, would arrive late and discover most of the seats tipped forward showing they were reserved. Mick simply ignored this and sat wherever he liked. We upset lots of groups of students and eventually one of the students realised that I shouldn't have been there in the first place. He told me that he was going to complain to the Bursar about what I was doing. I knew I was on a hiding to nothing so I backed off and didn't free-load anymore. Mick had the right to meals so he continued to upset the students but this time he did it on his own. He too lost the right to meals in his third year so he had to find alternative ways to feed himself that did not involve spending any money. He was cunning and sneaky and had no problem.

I was not so lucky. I had a girlfriend and, although I only saw her once or twice a week, it was always me that paid. She enjoyed going to Central London. I paid the bus fare. She enjoyed going to the theatre; guess who paid? She began to enjoy eating at Italian restaurants—she was lucky—I was always able to fork out for it. With this focus upon her costs I was always dreadfully short of money for anything else. The gas meter in my room ate the shilling coins as though they were chocolate buttons. My landlady had it set up so that she received a 'commission' from each coin. Her 'commission' worked out to be much better value than the gas I received. One morning I woke up and thought about breakfast. The gas was dead; I had used the gas to heat the room the previous evening and I had used up the shilling's worth. It was bitterly cold and a hot drink would have been so helpful to start the day. I checked my small food cupboard; I really was an optimist as I knew there was nothing in it. To my delight I'd missed a can stashed away at the back—I had a meal! My jubilation was short lived because it turned out that my surprise meal consisted of a tin of processed peas. My heart fell but it's amazing what hunger does for the appetite. I opened the tin, poured away the thick green watery solution and ended up with about three quarters of a tin of gray, green spheres. I ate them raw. It was the most memorable meal that I ate there. I can't say it was my favourite meal but it was certainly the one that is easiest to recall.

In our second and third years we both lived outside college but Mick had no definite place of his own. Sometimes he'd come back to my place for the night but usually he chose to stay in college. He simply broke into rooms and stayed there until morning. He didn't actually damage any windows or doors—he was far cleverer than that. His favourite haunt was the pottery room because, during the winter, he could turn the kiln on and keep warm.

No-one ever guessed that Mick was using the art room in this way. During the winter months the use of the kiln must have been fairly obvious to whomsoever taught in the pottery room but no-one made a fuss about it. Perhaps the warmth from the kiln added to the poor heat from the inadequate radiators and made the room comfortable. Mick's little 'crime' was actually benefitting the students.

Before he finished working at night he would carefully set one of the window catches so that, a quick glance by the grounds staff would suggest the windows were locked tight; although it appeared locked, it was in fact open. Late at night, after the groundsmen had done their lock-up and security patrols, he'd climb in and quietly make his 'bed' up. His bed was a long table that he dragged in front of the kiln and slept upon. He made sure he brought improvised bedding with him. He placed his feet near the open kiln to be kept nice and warm.

This was his favourite haunt but one day he found the locks on the windows had been replaced by a more secure variety. He could no longer leave the windows unlocked as the locks would not allow this subterfuge. The locks were either clearly unlocked or clearly locked. There was no means of making them fit his needs. Mick was desperate; he had to find another place to sleep. He walked around the college until he came to the block set aside for student study rooms. He noticed one window in the shower room was left open. He jumped up and grabbed the ledge and somehow he squeezed through the remarkably small opening. Mick showed me the window and I had to acknowledge that he had done remarkably well to slip through such a small opening. Mick was hardly athletic but the ends justified the means and he managed to overcome the obstacle. Once inside, he walked into one of the rooms and pulled cushions onto the floor and made his bed. I know this because one night, after a drink at the local pub, I didn't feel like the long walk home so I stayed in college with him, and we both got in the same way.

One day, whilst walking along a corridor in the student study block, Mick noticed a key in the lock of one of the office doors used by the lecturers. The lecturer of this particular office was sitting inside working at her desk. Mick pulled the door shut and pocketed the key. Mick was a dangerous soul and simply being with him made me an accomplice and partner in his crime. We rushed off immediately and heard the door of the office open as the surprised lecturer came out to investigate. Mick pulled at me and we spun on our heels and walked straight back towards her. As we passed, she asked if we had seen anyone near her door. Acting in complete innocence, Mick said he hadn't although he added that he had heard someone rushing down the stairs. She didn't mention the key—she had probably forgotten it was in the lock and didn't associate the door closing with the theft. This key meant Mick had a secure place to sleep at night—namely her office. He slept there for almost a term and no one but I ever knew a thing about it.

That room was actually next-door to the office of our personal tutor. Mick had stolen the key after our monthly chat with him. Once a month, we were expected to talk over our personal problems with him and he was to act as a 'friend' to help us and guide us through our college experience. Neither Mick nor I felt comfortable with this man. For some reason, Mick and I didn't like or trust him and, in the middle of our second year, we caused a minor uproar. Our tutor had invited us to a meeting, along with the rest of his 'flock', and we went along arriving noticeably late as usual. There was a very work-like atmosphere in the office as we entered and heads turned our way to witness our noisy and late invasion. The Christian Union students were all busy chatting about how they had problems with work and were receiving guidance about how to plan their studies and use their time effectively; Mick and I were not a part of this and had our usual chat between ourselves. This time the tutor asked us, in front of the others, if we had anything to talk to the group about. I said I had. I told him that Mick and I thought his tutorials were a total waste of everyone's time. I told him it was nothing personal—although it was; we simply found the meetings pointless. I told him we would not attend any more meetings in the future. A hush fell across the room as the 'proper' students witnessed our act of rebellion. We gave our personal tutor no time to react to my statement. In fact, we wasted no more of anyone's time—we just got up and walked out.

Understandably, our personal tutor was very offended by our action and very soon after he checked with our other lecturers and tried to get 'heavy' with us but we simply refused to go back. He decided to take the matter further and, in a written memo, he told us that we were to be sent to the Principal at some time in the near future for a dressing down. We waited but nothing happened. We had called his bluff and nothing came of it. We didn't have personal tutorials for the rest of our time in college. Our stand caused several more students to do the same but the rebellion was very short lived by them—we were the only ones who wouldn't cave in. I imagine we made it very uncomfortable for our personal tutor. It must have been hard in the staff common room trying to explain how two of his students simply wouldn't do anything he wanted.

Following his failure to get us to conform he probably kept very quiet about it to save his face and reputation. Fortunately our personal tutor didn't take us for any other lectures so the situation was very easy for us. We did bump into him a few times after our walkout and he always dodged aside to avoid us—that suited us fine. Our Education lecturer chatted to us about what we were doing; it was obvious that he had been asked to step in and try to help hold the line.

He listened to what we said and although he disapproved of our actions he didn't try to force the issue. In fact, he offered a compromise. If we needed any help we could go to him. Luckily for him, we never had to take up his offer. He was a very astute and kind man.

One night Mick broke into the study block and, because he was still feeling wide awake, he decided not to go to sleep immediately but do something else to pass the time. There were numerous books on the shelves but, as Mick was not really much of a reader, these did not grab his attention. Feeling rather at a loss he decided to improvise. He started playing his violin. He had little or no skill with this instrument and, when he played it in front of me, it made me think of a cat being tortured. There was a tiny flaw in Mick's plan. His impromptu concert was in the early hours of the morning and he really should have known better but, since caution meant nothing to him, his behaviour was in no way extraordinary. A grounds man was walking around the site to check on security and obviously heard the screaming, banshee-racket that Mick was making. There had been several thefts from this block and, since the playing was so bad, he thought kids were in there fooling around. He went in to investigate.

Very quietly he crept to the doorway of the room where Mick was and thrust the door open. Mick stopped and asked 'Oh, are you locking up now?' The grounds man said several unprintable things to Mick and then said he was going to report Mick to the Principal. Mick simply said he had walked in through an open door. The grounds man swore at Mick's obvious lying and Mick admitted it wasn't true but even so that's what he would say. The grounds man was in a dodgy situation. Who would the Principal believe? The whole 'professional' thing would force her to accept Mick's word and thus reprimand the grounds man. He would probably have lost his job into the bargain because the college administration was really hot on security (or so they thought).

The grounds man finally evicted Mick and told him he'd forget the incident but should Mick ever try to put something on him again he'd get more than he bargained for. He mentioned a 'few friends' outside college who quite enjoyed giving people 'lessons'. Mick had won this battle but it was a Pyrrhic victory for him because the building was always very secure after that. Mick also sensed that the threat for violent retribution was a real warning to watch his step. Although he had lost the room he didn't give up sleeping in the block. It was now a game of cat and mouse. Mick had to hide inside the building whilst it was being locked and this waiting in the building and hanging around for a long time before it was locked. The grounds men worked in pairs and cleared each floor from the top downwards. They never checked the toilet on the top floor properly. They certainly entered the toilet and checked the cubicles but they didn't check the cupboard that contained all the cleaning equipment. Mick had discovered that this cupboard could have its lock apparently secure when in fact it was unlocked. Mick just had to wait it out before emerging. There were no motion sensor alarms to worry about. It was a successful method but Mick did not enjoy the stress of waiting for so long in the dark, tiny cupboard.

At the beginning of our third year we were told to put our names down on lists for study rooms. The study rooms were in a large old block that stood majestically atop a hill—it overlooked the whole college. For one reason or another—actually it was nothing more than idleness and lack of organisation—we missed the lists and ended up with nowhere to work or relax during free time. We decided to gatecrash one of the rooms. We looked over the 'completed' lists and at random chose a room number. We walked up to it and entered. The female students who 'owned' it were very hostile but Mick shut them up by asking them if it was right for Christians to turn people away. I found his delivery dreadfully embarrassing but he knew his stuff; he gave them the whole works about the story of the Good Samaritan and what it meant to be a good practicing Christian—Oh boy, if there was a God I think he probably looked down in dismay at what Mick was doing. Being Christian Union types, the female students were in a dilemma. Basically they detested us for intruding upon their space but they were meant to forgive their enemies and turn the other cheek. They were pained by their inevitable conclusion as it meant their little retreat was no longer their own. To give them their due they did try to get on speaking terms with us but within two months Mick and I had the room to ourselves. One female tried to sit it out but she became isolated and had to give up her struggle as a lost cause. The previous occupants all managed to find spaces in more acceptable rooms with normal people and after a couple of months nobody mentioned it anymore.

The little room we had hijacked rapidly took on a life of its own and soon became a centre of attraction for all students who, like us, didn't fit in with the prevailing ethos of the college. On impulse I painted out one of the windows with an enormous cartoon character. Mick painted the other window and soon the room was in semi-darkness. The paint was thick powder based and when it dried it didn't let much light in. We had to have the main ceiling strip lights on all the time, even in bright sunlight. A couple of days after the painting we had a visitation from the college administration who told us we had to remove the paint and clean the windows. We professed ignorance of the painting and, as they had no proof it was us (who else could it have been?), we never did get around to cleaning it off. Within a few weeks the whole of the block became totally changed. All the windows were painted out. It seemed that in every room we had allies. Most of the windows were echoes of our own designs but some were quite imaginative. We had started our own guerrilla art exhibition. The college authorities dropped their heavy approach and quietly put-up with us. The problem had mushroomed beyond all proportions and any silly attempt to discipline us would have backfired rather badly.

We really got our own back on the Christian Union community because the whole of the floor we were on soon emptied until there were only the 'unsociables' and the liberally minded left. I was confronted by one Christian Union girl called Judy who asked me why I had done such nasty things. Why had I upset the administration? Why did I have long hair? Why was I noisy? Why did I insult the Christian Union so much? I didn't even try to answer her torrent of questions. She was very confused and I'm sure she prayed a great deal for my soul to be repaired, restored and returned to the 'pasture' et al. No-one pretended to understand why Mick did anything but they had hope that I would be more 'sensible'—I wasn't. Mick was so anti-everything except for the things he supported. He was a maverick and hard to predict. I just know that he hated all forms of authority. There was nothing better for him than causing a commotion. Private property and possessions seemed ridiculous and certainly weren't sacrosanct. His only reservation was his books that I mentioned earlier—he hated it when anyone opened a volume and caused a crease mark to appear upon the spine—that was unforgiveable.

Towards the end of the second year at college Mick suddenly started acting even more strangely and I collared him and asked him what was up. He told me that he'd almost been caught breaking into one of the rooms in which he sometimes slept. He had been halfway into the window when one of the patrolling grounds men had happened along. Mick had run off and then jumped on his bike. He had then ridden across the large lawns to make his escape. Arriving at the fence, that bordered the college grounds, he threw his bike over and then proceeded to get over himself. He was halfway over when his foot was grabbed. With a kick he got rid of the restraining hand but at the same time he lost his shoe. He had to pedal off into the night with only one shoe. He arrived at my place very late and I let him bring his bike in. The next day I went in to college and went up to the attic where he stored his things. I found a pair of his shoes and he was back in action. Mick was concerned that the threat of violence might happen; he had a few uncomfortable weeks looking over his shoulder as he left the college grounds. Nothing happened to him; he was lucky.

For a few nights he stayed at my place so as to let the coast clear a little. The grounds man confronted him a few days later. The grounds man knew it had been Mick because he had recognised him and the bike. This bicycle had very characteristic pedals. One of the cotter pins was loose and this meant that as Mick pedalled along the pedals made a clunk as they jerked unsteadily about on the cranks. He made slow progress because it was very difficult to co-ordinate both legs with the peculiar pedal situation. I imagine the grounds man followed Mick across the lawn following the 'clunk, clunk, clunk' as Mick made his getaway. Of course, Mick denied that it had been him and, since the grounds man had no substantial proof he couldn't really do anything. Even so it became very difficult for Mick to find any safe place to doss down and since he was in the middle of his exam courses he really needed somewhere stable where he could be based to work.

Fortune was to smile upon him. Mick had heard about a large abandoned reservoir that was teeming with many forms of animal wildlife and plants and thus a centre for conservationists and bird watchers. Mick discovered this reservoir one day whilst he was out and about on his scooter.

He immediately fell in love with the reservoir site and started spending a great deal of his time there. It wasn't long before he was noticed by a party of do-gooders. He was very soon co-opted into a local pressure group that was fighting the attempts of the local Council to close the place and level it and build on the reclaimed land. Mick was really angry about the imminent destruction of the site that would involve the brutal murder of so many animals. It wasn't long before Mick invited me to go with him to look at his new-found natural wonderland. The reservoir was indeed a derelict with huge chunks of concrete displaced from their proper locations. Mick told me it was the result of war damage; he was almost certainly correct. I couldn't imagine how such destruction could have taken place otherwise. The shifting of such enormous blocks would have meant incredible forces being applied—a doodlebug or two would have done it.

He was correct about the teeming wildlife; it was a haven. There was evidence of numerous mammals from the smallest voles up to and including badgers and foxes. Birdlife was abundant and Mick took great pleasure in showing me the discarded pellets from owls; the tiny furry bundles of poo contained fur and bones from numerous shrews and mice that didn't make it home. There was an abundance of life; the one group missing was fish. This location was a huge reservoir but there was nothing swimming around beneath the surface. There was a simple reason for this. There was hardly any water. The bomb damage had caused large cracks in the bottom of the reservoir effectively destroying any ability to hold water—rain water was collected in large quantities but as soon as it drained to a low point it simply drained away through the tremendous cracks. There were a few isolated pools and the swans had made one their home;

their pool was dwarfed by the expanse of broken concrete surrounding it—an oasis amid the concrete.

One day, whilst looking around and stopping the local kids from throwing bricks at the swans, Mick was approached by a man who started talking to him. The chap who was questioning Mick turned out to be someone rather important—an MBE. He was a local bigwig with a huge interest in preserving the abandoned reservoir as a nature reserve. He asked Mick if he would help guard the batch of swan's eggs that had been laid that very same day. Of course, Mick agreed immediately, and only found out later that he was being expected to sleep alongside the nest every night—the MBE and his other cronies were much too busy to do that sort of thing themselves. Mick agreed to become a guard and that night began sleeping in a small tent on the bank of the reservoir. Ten yards away, on a small concrete island, the swans were trying to rear their brood in peace.

Of course, Mick soon found that he had taken on more than he had thought and his college work was suffering. The travelling back and forth was expensive and very time-consuming and Mick, although a dedicated preserver of animal life, really wanted to pass his examinations and become a teacher. Mr. MBE came up with the solution by suggesting Mick should stay in the house of his next-door neighbour. Mick went along to this place and knocked on the door. He was surprised to see someone come out looking remarkably like himself. This man turned out to be a biologist who wrote and illustrated books on nature.

The house, though huge, was full of magazines and periodicals on every biological subject imaginable. In one corner, by the door, was a box full of 'gifts' for the local charity. These gifts were unwanted books sent to the man to be reviewed. He thought himself a splendid type because he gave them away for nothing. He told Mick that he could stay upstairs and showed Mick several large rooms that were his to use. The rooms were huge and would have been a marvellous place to live but for the stench of damp stale paper—the whole house reeked of it. The reason for the smell was simple; the roof was in an awful state of disrepair and the upper floor ceilings all showed evidence of water damage. The paper littering the house absorbed the moisture like sponges and thus the damp atmosphere. It was stupid because the house owner loved the nooks and magazines and yet he was doing nothing whatsoever to preserve them properly.

At first Mick got on admirably with the house owner. During the day he went to college and in the evening he did the man's garden. Night was spent as usual over at the swan's nest. I was invited over to see the new place and I arrived just as Mick was finishing his clean-up of the garden. I was invited in by the owner and led through the alleys of mouldy paper and out into the back garden. I found Mick at the extreme end of the garden cutting back stinging nettles and weeds. He told me the whole garden, which was about twenty yards by forty, had been overwhelmed by wild plants. He had spent several weeks getting it into a proper state and he certainly had the beginnings of his efforts showing. Already seeds he had planted were breaking through and there promised to be a luxurious growth of more desirable plants quite soon. He had cut back overgrown hedges and exposed the many interesting plants that had been overwhelmed beneath the rampant foliage. I was very impressed by his efforts and results—not only was he knowledgeable but he was skilled in the application of gardening techniques and the nurturing of plants.

He was just about finished for the day so we both went up to see his flat—he had invited me over for a meal. I was horrified at the state of things in his room. Mick had been living in the rooms for some time and had plenty of time to tidy it up. I refused to eat a thing until we cleared some of the mess. It was a mammoth task and I told Mick that he had to buy a few things to make the work possible. We popped out to the local shop and bought cleaning items and a couple of pairs of rubber gloves. Only one pair of gloves was used; Mick was amused at my squeamishness, he stood back whilst I washed the mountain of filthy crockery and dishes. I looked at the saucepans and had to wash them as well because they seemed to have accumulated about thirty years of grease. Once started on the road to cleanliness it was difficult to stop and I was soon washing out cupboards and the stove and the sink and the draining board—you name it I washed it! It took me a couple of hours hard slog before I felt 'safe' eating there. I had to do the toilet as well—that was also unbelievably horrible. My hard work in cleaning it turned it from a nasty shade of brown to a gleaming white—you could even read the name of the manufacturer.

Having finished my cleaning, we both walked around to the local butcher's, and bought some meat—Mick had no qualms about eating meat despite his ecological and 'power-to-animal' views. We picked up some potatoes and vegetables and I thought we were set for a good feast. It turned out to be rather a mean meal because he had no salt, pepper, or gravy or spices at. The meal was tasteless and I never took up any more offers to eat there. I had never actually cooked a proper meal myself and had no idea about herbs and spices and the other tricks one used to make food tasty. I must have watched my mother cook a thousand times without actually noticing what she was doing. Mick also invited me to stay the night; in the tent at the reservoir. My earlier experiences 'on-the-road' with him were more than enough to make me refuse his generous offer.

Having finished the garden, the owner of the property suddenly demanded that Mick should now start repairing the house—the place was rotten with neglect and would have needed a large team of skilled workers to repair it in anything less than six months. Mick didn't have any building skills and had no inclination to do such work. Mick took a stand; he told the owner that he was only staying there to look after the swan's eggs and he certainly wasn't a servant or a slave. The owner was furious and demanded that Mick obey him—really. This set the seal and Mick refused to do anything—he wouldn't even speak to the owner anymore.

By sheer coincidence, Mick was unable to get back to look after the eggs the night after the dispute with his 'landlord'. Vandals noted his absence and smashed the eggs by throwing stones at the nest. Mick discovered the tragedy the next evening when he turned up for his duty. Since the focus of his life had disappeared—the eggs were smashed, Mick was no longer under the influence of the house owner. Up until that point all the conservation group had been putting pressure on Mick to do more and more for them—they of course, were too busy with their important lives. They exploited him so brazenly and used his love of wildlife to get him to do their bidding. The smashing of the eggs changed all that and Mick was freed of his self-imposed bonds. He got great pleasure out of telling the conservation group that he was leaving and that they could do it themselves in future. There was never such a horrified group of well-to-dos. To think what they had done for him, and this was the way he treated them—you never can trust the lower classes.

Mick moved out of the house when the owner suddenly demanded several weeks rent for the time Mick had lived there. No mention of rent had ever taken place—in fact Mick had stayed there solely to be an egg guardian. Mick had cleared the garden because he enjoyed working with plants. The man said this was rubbish—in fact Mick was nothing more than a lodger. Mick left immediately and went back to 'dossing' down on the floors at the college.

Soon after quitting, Mick received a letter at college; it was from the owner of the house telling him that, unless he paid up, he would be taken to court and prosecuted for the money. Mick took this to the Principal at college and despite her dislike of Mick she saw the injustice about to be set upon him. Accordingly she instructed the college solicitor to write a reply on Mick's behalf. It was explicit and filled with warnings that any attempt to prosecute Mick would be challenged by the college. The matter died there and then.

There was one other funny incident that took place whilst he was living near the reservoir. His old scooter was flaking out and needed a grave. He chose to dump it by pushing it into the Thames but, being crafty, he reported it as missing and the local police took the particulars. I asked Mick why he had done this; he had no insurance so he couldn't make a claim. Mick told me that he had just arranged insurance at an address he was using anonymously. I wasn't quite sure what he was up to but it sounded very suspicious.

Unfortunately, his cunning scheme came apart. Soon after the scuttling of his scooter Mick was horrified to see it lying open to all eyes in the mud. It was a very low tide and the scooter was left high and dry and very visible.

Mick raced to the police station and reported the fact that he'd seen a scooter that 'might' have been his and he told them where it was. Their reaction was totally unexpected. They told him to arrange to get it out because it was a danger to river users. Mick said he would 'if it was his' and left. He went back to the spot and pushed the thing even further out into the riverbed until it was covered again—the police probably didn't expect this sort of 'rescue'. Mick decided that he had better forget the claim for his scooter because it might have got complicated. He was well rid of that scooter though I can't say I really approved of where he left it. I wonder if it ever becomes visible during freaky low tides—anyone want a scooter?

I know where there is a really good one up for grabs. It won't cost you a penny. It may require a little restoration to repair some minor water damage.

All through my first two years at college I had been living in my bedsit. I met some people like myself in a pub and over a period of about a year I had become quite friendly with them. One of them heard about a flat that was empty and I was invited to move in with them. I jumped at the chance. The thought of sharing with them sounded really good and the rent was hardly more than what I was paying for one lousy room. As I was moving out of my place and getting rid of rubbish I mentioned the move to Mick. He expressed an interest in my old place and I told him he could move in if he wished.

He was very grateful and said he'd cook dinner for me. I knew he had no place to live so I asked him where he was going to cook. He told me to meet him in the coffee bar at college at midday on Sunday and he'd surprise me. I did as he suggested and I was surprised. He took me along to the college kitchens where the meals were prepared for the six hundred or so students and lecturers. He opened several cupboards and took out boxes of this and boxes of that and various foodstuffs. In a huge vat was a vast quantity of prepared chips submerged in water. They were ready to be cooked for the meal the following day.

Mick scooped out two large portions and then turned on the gas of the fryer. This was as big as a bath and filled with cooking oil. The gas roared and the oil started to heat. It took about half an hour for the bath of oil to heat up enough for the chips to be put in. It became very warm in the kitchen as the oil reached the right temperature. Mick found a small metal sieve to place the chips in and he then put it into the vat. It looked ridiculous because it was so tiny compared to the size of the vat. I was very worried about being caught but Mick was full of reassurances because he said he did it every Sunday, when he was in college, and he hadn't been caught in all the time he'd been doing it. The meal was O.K. and afterwards he opened up the dessert store and soon made about a gallon of Instant Whip; Mick had no way of measuring the quantities he kept adding more milk and more powder until he got the consistency he desired. Unfortunately, we had far more than we needed—and, to tell the truth, it was horrible.

After eating we washed up, to hide traces of our crime, and left. This was one of the few occasions when I saw Mick clean crockery and utensils properly—but, he had a vested interest. Mick had filled a large cardboard box with tins and other food items for eating during the next week. He continued supplementing his diet in this way until we left college, over a year later. No-one but me ever knew a thing about his 'lunches'. I wonder what the kitchen staff made of it. Didn't they notice the continual losses to the stock?

CHAPTER 6

Bedsitter Images

Mick moved into my old place and was soon well at home there. It was a dreadful slum and I had hated my time spent in the appalling house. The landlady was an obnoxious Irish woman who laid down stringent rules about what was permissible and what was not. She made it particularly clear that no women were to stay the night. I really hated that woman and detested meeting her once every month to pay the rent—it was three pounds a week, which probably seems negligible, but when one considers the state of the place that was daylight robbery. She lived in a large house near to my parents. I loathed going there and handing over my money. The house was full of expensive 'tat'—she wore fluffy pink slippers. Although I was from a very working class background I had acquired enough education to notice tackiness when I saw it. A lot of money had been spent on rubbish.

I had one single room, which was meant to be a bedsitter—it was a slum. The toilet was upstairs and I shared it with a motley crowd who came and went during my stay there. The bath was a filthy brown with the stain of rust that was left behind by the water that dripped from the monstrous water heater. I never had a bath there because I didn't trust the boiler—I expected it to explode at any moment. I tried cleaning the bath once; it was a futile effort as the staining had penetrated into the enamel of the bath itself. No-one else bothered so once was more than enough.

The toilet seat was made of cracked yellow plastic. Unfortunately it was so badly stained that it looked brown rather than yellow. It took very little imagination to understand the discolouration. This undesirable colour change made sitting on it unthinkable and always reminded me of the poem found on endless factory and pub walls

"It's no good standing on the seat
Crabs in this place jump six feet"

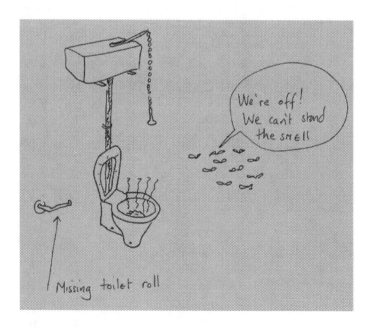

Whenever I was forced to use the toilet I wrapped yards of tissue round the seat in the hope of preventing infection. I never caught anything so my precautions were obviously effective. I had made the mistake of leaving toilet rolls in the bathroom. They always disappeared; what on earth did anyone want with toilet rolls? They simply disappeared. The toilet rolls didn't cost me anything; I 'borrowed' them from college. I just got irritated that no-one else ever bought any and mine always disappeared as soon as I left them.

There was a room next to the toilet and for months I had heard funny noises coming from behind the partition wall. The section that was partitioned off was just about large enough to hold a small single bed—which in fact it did. On this bed slept a tramp-like character. He did jobs around the houses owned by the landlady and in gratitude she let him exist in the wardrobe-sized space. He was incredibly filthy and usually drunk to insensibility. He was another reason for not using the toilet! In two years I only saw him a couple of times although I heard him come in lots of times. In his drunken state he would collide with the walls as he made his way along the corridor outside my room. Then he'd walk up the stairs crashing his feet down as he staggered upwards.

While I was there two attractive young women moved in and I bumped into them one morning and in my neighbourly way I said hello to them. I met them a few days later and this time we chatted briefly at the front door. They seemed friendly and interesting. One of them was pushing a buggy and the other was standing alongside her. They were very attractive in their mini-skirts. A few days later I bumped into them again and we passed some time talking about important things like the weather. We parted, they went upstairs to their room and I went into my cell. A few minutes later, one of them came down stairs and knocked on my door. I opened it and the mother asked me if I would look after her baby for a few minutes whilst they went down the road to the shops. I thought she was taking a bit of a risk as she didn't know me at all but I said I didn't mind and said I'd do it for her. She said her baby was asleep and asked me to come upstairs to her flat so she could show me where things were—just in case. I followed her upstairs and couldn't help but notice that she had very nice legs and a decidedly attractive bum—for goodness sake—I was about twenty years old and my blood was filled with hormones of the type that get you excited.

I was given a cup of coffee as I was shown where the baby things were and then the two women left me. They returned after only a few minutes so I didn't have any problems at all. We started chatting and I quickly learned that they were both married to men who were serving several years in the local prison. Both of the women mentioned the fact that they got really bored and frustrated. One of them reached down to the side of the sofa and passed me a small magazine. I had seen this on the top shelf in newspaper shops—it was Forum; a sex magazine. I was asked if I ever read it or magazines like it. I told them that I hadn't seen it before—a lie—and that I never really thought about sex very much—a huge lie—I thought of little else most of the time. I didn't know whether or not they were just teasing me but I made an excuse and made my exit. I suppose I could have gone along with them and played a game or two but one factor certainly held me back. Both of their husbands were in prison for violent offences; I didn't wish to be on their hit-list when they got out. I'm afraid I left the two young women as bored and frustrated as they had been before our chat—what a silly boy!

Actually there was another curious incident like this just before I moved out of the hovel. I was on a bus and a drunken woman got on and she was unable to operate the automatic ticket-dispensing machine. The bus was already in motion and the driver seemed oblivious of her plight—or maybe he knew exactly what he was doing. The poor soul was tossed back and forth in accordance with the motion of the bus. She was dressed nicely and very attractively; I thought she was probably in her mid-thirties—quite old really considering how boyishly young I was.

Since I was the only person on the bus (besides the driver of course) I went over to help her. I offered my arm and she took it. She thrust some coins into my hand and asked me to put it in the slot for her. I gave her back the spare coins and she managed to put them back into her purse. I gave her the ticket that had popped out of the slot and helped her negotiate her way through the automatic turnstile. As she passed through to the other side she grabbed a hold of my arm and I was dragged to a seat at the back of the bus. Then, once seated, she leaned over me and told me I was lovely. Her breath was heavy with the smell of alcohol. I thanked her for her compliment. She managed to focus for a moment as she spoke again and asked me if I would like to go to bed with her. Astonished, I thanked her but said 'I'm sorry but my mother's expecting me'. This was the first thing that came into my head but it was enough to get me out of her grasp. I could have been her temporary toy-boy—at least for one night. I don't think she was a working girl although I was so inexperienced I probably couldn't tell anyway. Perhaps she had just taken a fancy to her young knight in shining armour. I may have missed a great opportunity. Hmmm . . . maybe not!

Exactly one week later I was waiting for a bus when a car pulled up at the bus stop. The man inside asked if anyone knew the way to a place about four miles away. No-one else in the queue responded—they were more worldly wise than me. I pointed the direction, which was simply straight ahead. The driver seemed to be uncertain and asked if I was going that way. I said yes and he offered me a lift. I thought it was better than waiting for a bus and so I got in.

We had driven perhaps a hundred yards when he turned to me and said 'I suppose you get offered lots of lifts don't you?' I said no. He then asked me what I thought of photography. I said I didn't really think a great deal about it. He then passed several postcards to me and asked me to have a look at them. I did. They were all very erotic indeed and showed all manner of incredible goings on. There were all possible permutations depicted on those few snaps. He asked me what I thought of them and I said 'Nothing at all really'. This obviously disappointed him but unabashed he asked me if I liked blue films. I said no and said I thought they were boring and lacked any artistic value. Fortunately this conversation had lasted sufficiently long enough for me to reach where I lived. I told him to stop, which he did, and as I got out he invited me to his place for a 'party'. I declined his invitation and left. He immediately drove away. He drove about fifty yards on and then did a quick U-turn and headed back the way we had come. I suppose he was out to try his luck again. Perhaps he had more success next time. The photographs I had been shown had displayed both genders cavorting so I am not sure whether he was gay, bisexual or just weird. I never found out—thank goodness. It was peculiar having these two 'sexual' experiences together like that. Neither of them was run of the mill. Maybe Mick was right, maybe it was the way I walked.

Mick moved in to my hovel but I continued to pay the rent ensuring that the landlady didn't know of the new arrangement. I hated doing this because I wanted nothing to do with the 'ratbag' but I couldn't let him down. Now and then she used to pop around to check up on things. She used to ask him how I was—she never twigged that I had moved out even though Mick lived there for just about a year. She was pretty stupid. She complained once about me using sticky tape to hang posters up on the walls. I said I had a special method of removing the tape so that it left no marks—she believed it. Of course when I took my posters down I simply ripped the tape off the paper and made large rectangular tear marks. Actually the paper was well beyond its useful life and God alone knows where she found it. She couldn't possibly have chosen it (or then again perhaps she could).

A few weeks after Mick moved in, he told me that he had a pet. I asked him what he meant but he took his time to elaborate. He gave me a history of how he had discovered it. He awoke one morning and noticed looping shiny trails across the threadbare carpet. He traced the trails and found they led back under the ancient gas stove. Looking under it he saw a stationary slug. Delighted with this little companion he decided to feed it. Every morning he put down lettuce leaves for it. The man was bloody mad but he thought his pet was great. Every morning the carpet would bear new tracings left behind after the night moves of the slug—this only stopped when he trod on the unfortunate creature one morning. An old friend bit the dust.

Despite the squalor Mick really liked that place. He was always at home in a mess. He always disorganised his life to make everything flow awkwardly. He hated efficiency.

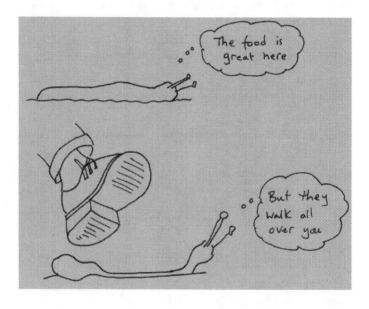

In the summer at the end of our second year in college, Mick decided to get a job in one of the local factories. He needed the money, as did we all, to tide him over till the next term began in September. He managed to get fixed up in a factory that made plastic models that was barely half a mile away from where he lived. He only managed to stay there a couple of weeks. He quit and told me awful stories of the incredible oppression and noise and, knowing Mick's outlook, I rather doubted that things were quite as bad as that. Simon was also working in the factory and since his parental home was miles away he decided to stay with Mick for the duration of the job. The bed-sit room was tiny and Simon slept in a sleeping bag on the floor. He certainly wasn't going to share a bed with Mick and repeat the terror of the experience on the field trip. He only managed to stay with Mick for a week because he found the situation intolerable. He didn't really like Mick playing the recorder at three o'clock in the morning. The thing that eventually moved him out was a mistake but even so it shocked him right down to his socks. Simon awoke one morning and heard Mick cleaning his teeth. This was really odd because Mick never cleaned his teeth; in fact he said cleaning one's teeth caused them damage. Simon listened to the sound of bristles on gums and put two and two together; his brain exploded in panic as he realised that Mick was using his brush! Leaping up he grabbed his clothes, got dressed and left, never to return. Mick told him afterwards that he had actually been using his own brush but the mere thought of Mick's mouth around the bristles was too much and Simon stayed away. Mick thought him pathetic and childish for worrying over such a minor event. I'm not so sure though; the thought of Mick using my toothbrush makes me shiver as well.

Having quit the factory Mick still needed money. He decided to visit some of his old acquaintances in the park that he'd worked in before the job at the school. He asked for a temporary job and was accepted on the spot—they really admired Mick. He loved the work because it meant tending the flowers and shrubs that adorned the section facing the road. Mick took particular pride in making the most public part of the park as presentable as possible. He was so different with plants. In his own life he lived in a mess but his plants were always so well tended.

On sunny days he took it very easy and often used to creep under the shrubs and bushes to lie in wait for some unsuspecting person out for a quiet walk. As they passed he would make funny noises and frighten them. No one ever came into the bushes to investigate—what an absurd thought! Also, during this time Mick started his hobby of making olde (yes) musical instruments. He found a piece of London plane timber that had fallen down from a tree and from this fragment he carved a replica of an old stringed instrument unlike anything I've ever seen. He got the design from an old illustration in one of his books. When he finished it, it looked wonderful but since Mick had no musical talent he was unable to play it. It was a great tribute to his skills as a non-musical artist.

As soon as we went back to college I was asked by Mick if I fancied sharing a house with him and several other people from our college. I said I wanted to see what the place was like first. Mick said there wasn't any place at the moment but he was looking. He took me out a couple of times on his scooter to look places over. One place remains firmly in my mind. It was a large house in Fulham that had been empty for a long time. For Mick it was a perfect squat—at least that was the impression I got from him before he actually showed it to me.

I have never seen such a wreck in my life. The house had been gutted. There were no water pipes (this was no problem for Mick—or so he said) and the toilet and bath were lying on the floor in broken, jagged pieces. Most of the ceiling was conveniently resting on the floor. I suppose it was easier to paint if it was underfoot as opposed to stretching upwards to reach it. Mick led me through the house remarking how it would be simple to tidy it up—I was thinking more along the lines of pulling it down to erect a slum in its place, at least a slum had water. I was convinced of the futility of the place when we came into the toilet. Actually it wasn't the 'official' toilet but people had obviously designated it as such. Piles of human excrement littered the floor and pools of urine wound their way lazily across, and through, the floorboards. Even Mick was taken aback by the shit and since I walked out, without so much as a word, he sensed that I wasn't going to even consider it.

Back at college, I told the other potential squatties about the place and they all backed out. The idea of sharing with Mick went completely out of their heads. They thought that the simple fact that he could even consider living under those conditions said something about him that they hadn't been aware of. Mick was rather upset that everyone backed out and I suppose I had done the dirty on him. Then again, he was prepared to do the dirty on us. We were only protecting ourselves—we didn't fancy getting dysentery just to keep Mick happy. Thus he had to look elsewhere and as usual he had absolutely no problem about conning his way into a cushy set-up.

It was during this summer that he met Katie. He was on holiday and touring the West Country again on his replacement scooter—touring around just like he had done with me (he was on his own this time, though.) As he turned a bend he noticed a couple of people standing forlornly alongside a motorbike. He pulled up—his brakes were working on this holiday and he asked if there was a problem and if they needed any help. They did. They had a flat tyre and no repair kit and, since it was miles from any town they were well and truly lumbered. Mick clambered off his scooter and got out his tools and repair kit and set to the task of repairing the offending tyre. Both of them stood back and let him get on with it. He finished fairly quickly and they chatted away together for a while asking each other what they were doing. Mick learned that they, too, were on holiday and also touring around as he was. They prepared to leave but before they did Mick told them to call in at his place in London if they were ever up that way. None of them had pencil or paper and so Mick found a piece of stone and a broken tile and scratched his address onto it. They parted ways and though they had been friendly, Mick didn't really expect them to take up his offer.

He forgot all about the encounter until several weeks after he had returned home. There was a knock at his door and he found, to his amazement, that the woman of the pair was on his doorstep. He looked round for the male companion but he wasn't to be seen. Katie said hello and that she was on her own—the bloke had been a friend and not a boyfriend. Invited in, Mick treated her to a meal and then had his way; or rather they had their way with each other. Thus began the romance of Mick and Katie—Katie 'with the smiling eyes'. She received this name from a piece of copper enamelling that Mick made in his third year. It was a piece of copper plate about four inches square and the design, though well drawn out and glazed was far too sentimental. Mick was very proud of this despite the universal disapproval by others who had seen his better work—even Katie thought it a bit syrupy. He made up for this setback though because he then painted a portrait of her face. It was solely from memory. The work only measured about nine inches by six but it was exceedingly good. The texture of the paint was curious—it didn't look like he had used a brush. I asked him how he had got the effect. He told me he had awoken one morning with a desperate urge to paint the portrait but he only had tubes of paint—he had nothing to apply it with. Puzzled I asked him how he had done it and was told that he had got the urge to do it early on the previous Sunday morning. He raced to the local paper shop; it was closed. He felt desperate for a short while because the need to paint her had become an obsession. He went back home and looked around for something that might work like a brush. He couldn't see anything that would help. The toothbrush seemed to be his only option but it didn't suit his needs.

His answer was staring back at him from the side of the gas stove. There, sitting amid the chaos of dirty crockery, lay his salvation. He saw a box of matches. He pulled one out and chewed the end until it was soft and mushy. He squeezed some paint onto a plate and stirred the chewed end into it. The fibrous end accepted paint readily and was easy to work with. Each match had a rather short life but, since he had a plentiful supply, he managed to complete the painting in one session.

As Mick was strange so was Katie peculiar. She was a perfect partner for him because she had complimentary eccentricities of her own. They were both 'Christians' but they were the only two signed-up members of their particular creed. It was very selfish and self-centred. For example, they planned to have a large family and, when I asked them how they could justify this on account of the world population explosion, I was told that their children would be 'special' and would go out and help make the world a better place. They really thought that they were both members of 'Homo Superior'—in fact, they were two hopelessly naive muddle-heads. I was surprised to discover that Katie was a doctor; though the thought of placing my life in her hands gave me feelings of great uncertainty. She was very timid and her lack of self-confidence impacted upon everything she did. In only one area of her life did she seem to have a surety of purpose—Mick was a rock for her to stand upon. The fact that she had tracked him down after the brief meeting suggested she saw something remarkable in him. They seemed to be made for each other and had been lucky enough to meet up.

Katie owned a Mini and drove it very badly indeed. She seemed unaware of the car being tossed back and forth by her poor application of accelerator and brakes. Being a passenger was like being tied onto a dodgem. The car accelerated and decelerated viciously and the brakes squealed a concerto of pain every time they were applied. She took no heed of other road users—they seemed invisible to her. Perhaps she was touting for clients by increasing the number of road accidents and bumping up the number of injured parties requiring hospital treatment. Of course, the inevitable happened and she ended up in hospital—the victim of her own bad driving. Mick was absolutely heartbroken when he heard of her plight but, since her injuries were only light, he soon recovered his equilibrium. Her car was a write-off though and she had been so shaken by the crash that she didn't drive again for some time.

Separately, they were curious but together they often became ridiculous. I was told of their regular habit of praying after making love. I'd heard this line before when he had done the wicked deed with the Jehovah's Witness—I thought this was the end for Katie. Mick elaborated and told me that they were so guilty because they weren't married that they used to pray for forgiveness after their fornication. I formed a gruesome image in my mind of the two of them in bed—panting and sweating after their efforts and then asking for forgiveness. I told Mick I thought he was being daft and Mick was really hurt by my comment—but I didn't feel able to lie to him about it. I had a very jaundiced view of marriage and saw no reason to believe it could be positive for Mick and Katie.

Katie recovered and it was not long afterwards when he came to me and told me that everything was okay now because they were married. Since I'd seen him the previous evening and it was still barely ten o'clock in the morning I asked how he managed to get it done so quickly. He told me he'd got married the previous night. They had been lying in bed and decided that enough was enough and that they simply had to marry. Mick had found an old ring and they went through the marriage ceremony together, having mouthed the words they pronounced themselves married. Remember that these two adults were both over thirty. He was almost a teacher and she was already a qualified doctor. It made me wonder what the professional types in England were made of—but they were serious. They were now married—they didn't need the blessing of society to confirm that. In a small way I admired their individual solution but, really, they were bonkers.

Now that he was married, Mick needed a proper home for Katie and he decided to rent a house with her. In the short term he had a problem. Where could he put her? It was at this time that one of the buildings in college became haunted. Students would swear that they heard strange noises coming from the roof space above one of the student dormitories. The block in question had a huge attic space running the entire length of the building. It was floored but it had no lighting. It had entrances at either end at the top of a short flight of stairs. Several students refused to sleep in their rooms until the 'ghosts' were dealt with. It fell onto the shoulders of one of the groundsmen to venture up into the unknown to sort out the problem. He made his way up without any problem and after unlocking the door he made his way along the roof space. The attic was stacked with all manner of discarded items that had been stacked away over the previous years. He didn't get very far when he heard a noise. The students who had complained had been correct. He continued with his exploration and stopped again when he heard more noise. He pointed his torch along the attic and suddenly caught movement in the light. He saw a ghostly apparition of a woman in a flowing white gown rushing around madly. He had had enough. He bolted away in the opposite direction.

The ghost disappeared and students returned to their rooms. The unintentional exorcism had worked. It was only later that Mick explained what had really happened. He had stolen a key to the attic and he had cleared a space for Katie. On the odd occasions she came over he would take her into the building and they'd sleep over in the attic. On the occasion of the ghost scene she had been there on her own. She had been rushing around because she had been terrified—she had thought there was a ghost. She had grabbed her few possessions and a sheet and rushed out wearing it like a flowing robe. No wonder the grounds man thought he'd seen a spirit.

Katie disappeared for a while as she had things to sort out. She left Mick to his own devices and would pop back when she was able to find time away from her job. Being a GP put constraints upon her trips. He rose to the challenge at once. He simply walked into an estate agent's and told them he was a senior lecturer at the local college—he needed a house temporarily. The estate agent was completely taken in; he was satisfied as to Mick's background and delighted to have such an important person on their books. Mick was given a fantastic house at a ridiculous rent—almost no rent at all. The house belonged to a religious man who was currently out in Africa on missionary work. Whilst away doing his good deeds, he wanted his house not so much rented out as lived in and cared for. Mick was told that he wasn't allowed to let anyone move in with him. Mick, in his role of lecturer had no problem agreeing to the simple terms.

And so he moved in—it was a fantastic place. It was huge and roomy with extensive gardens to the front and rear. Its huge beautiful bay windows overlooked extensive mature gardens. The house had been wonderfully maintained. It had warmth and light and certainly enough room for lots of people, which was Mick's plan anyway. In his wanderings, Mick came across many characters and several were offered the opportunity of staying in his house at a competitive rent. The rent he charged wasn't excessive but, since he let a large number of people staying, he was soon raking in a large profit. I told him I didn't approve of this blatant exploitation and our friendship was very strained because of this—I never felt quite as easy towards him after that. I thought he had gone too far and he was taking too many people for a ride. The people he invited back to his place were a very strange collection and varied enormously from the hippies who were 'into-drugs-man' and the creep who was into wife bashing. Visits to his new home were always interesting and I found myself at odds with Mick more and more.

Mick was ripping them off—his rent for the whole property was minimal but he didn't get it all his own way. His gas meter was broken into repeatedly—one time, it was fixed and then broken into the same day—obviously with little financial gain. It was the hippies. They had no need of money. They were unemployed and thus the meter was their sole income for buying their dope so they could escape the pressure. Mick was the real dope though, because he allowed them to continue like this, over and over again. He justified their behaviour by saying that they 'needed' to do it and thus he was doing them a service. He was looking after them; he was the guardian. I suppose that makes sense if one sees it as an attempt by Mick to run a commune although it had to make a tidy sum for him in the process.

Unfortunately the hippies were cruising and their antics mushroomed as they became more at home there. One day, Mick walked in the front door and the smell of dope almost blew him back out again. He went upstairs to have a look and found several of his hippie chums lying stretched out on mattresses. The mattresses had been taken from every bed in the house and piled onto the floor to make a whole new surface. They had simply ripped them off the beds and left piles of blankets and sheets on the floor. Mick was unable to get any order out of the mess; he took it on the chin—actually, they gave him some dope and he lit up and took off with them. I don't think he ever cleared up the mess and the mattresses never found their way back to their beds—they were too filthy for sleeping on anyway.

A few weeks later he came back and found a pile of sawn off furniture legs piled up against the front door. They were from the furniture in the house. Mick discovered that in their drugged state, the lodgers had sawn through every leg on all the items of furniture. They wanted everything on a lower level. Everything was now suitable for reaching whilst lying prone on the floor. This was a bit too much and Mick decided they had gone too far—he had standards? He kicked them out because of it. They were very ill-tempered about their eviction and took half the furniture with them whilst Mick was out. It was a pity that their gentleness and love and peace had produced nothing but squalor. I looked on with my own political perspective and was disapproving. Our friendship was slipping.

Having learnt his lesson Mick decided he really needed a young married couple with a baby or two—surely they would be more reasonable and trustworthy. A couple of weeks later, whilst visiting a post office, he happened to bump into a couple with a baby. They looked rather depressed and Mick asked what the problem was. Learning of their housing problem he invited them to come and stay with him. They accepted his offer to check out the house and, having seen it, they accepted Mick's offer of renting some rooms. They moved in and it seemed everything settled down and become quite relaxed and peaceful.

Mick noticed that when they moved in they had very few possessions except for a couple of large bath towels and half a dozen nappies. They had only one child so he thought that they would be able to cope well enough with just that few items. They were very hard up but Mick's rent was manageable. They kept themselves to themselves and Mick had no problem with them.

A peculiar smell started percolating and wafting through the house and investigation seemed to indicate that it was coming from the rooms occupied by the couple. Mick was reluctant to burst into their rooms and so he left it for a few days. It was hot weather and the smell was becoming unbearable. One afternoon he noticed several flies crawling out from under the door of the offending room. He opened the door and took a look. The whole room was covered in flies and the smell was overwhelming. The walls were covered beneath a living mass of flies—obviously attracted by the smell. He opened the large window and a mass of flies escaped immediately but a huge number remained walking on the floor, walls and ceiling. Fetching a vacuum cleaner he sucked the creatures up as best he could. Afterwards he emptied their bodies onto the garden (Remember he didn't like killing things—so this task was very difficult for him).

When the couple came in later, Mick told them about it and asked what was causing the smell. They didn't seem to know but they said they would clean the room out immediately to see what it was. Nothing happened though. At this time Mick noticed that some of his towels were missing and, since there was no one else in the house except the couple, he knew they must have them. The smell worsened until Mick was unable to stand it any longer. He went into the room and started looking for the cause. There had to be something responsible for the vile smell. He found it almost immediately; the smell seemed to be coming from the wardrobe. He went into the room and started looking for the cause. He found it immediately. He pulled open the doors and inside he found a rotting pile of filthy nappies. Once the nappies had been used they had been slung in the wardrobe. Mick also noticed that the couple's bath towels had been ripped up and these too had served as nappies and were part of the filthy pile. He also found his towels. They had been ripped up and had served the same fate.

When the couple came in Mick confronted them and asked what they thought they were doing and told them to do something about it immediately. They were very apologetic and she took them all upstairs into the bathroom to wash. Mick could hear her splashing water into the bath. The nappies were all thrown into the bath to soak; they hadn't been rinsed so all the solids rose to the surface as a scum. The couple went out leaving them to soak. I called round that afternoon and whilst talking to Mick I noticed the vile smell inside the house. Mick told me the details above. We went upstairs to the bathroom and the shitty water was running out through the overflow. The smell was unbelievable; I almost vomited when I saw the corruption inside the bath.

Mick was unable to see the couple about this business because he had commitments in college. He came home a few days later and they had made their exit taking some of the things from the house. There weren't many because the hippies had already done a pretty good job of stripping the house bare themselves. Mick was irritated by one thing though; they had taken all the rest of his towels. I suppose it was only fair because they'd left all of their towels behind (yes, they were still in the bath—Mick had simply shut the door on that problem) This second negative experience convinced Mick that sharing was rather out of the question and for the rest of his stay there he was alone—he found it much easier.

Mick now had the house to himself and he soon settled down into his own routines. Katie was on the scene occasionally but I rarely saw her. It was at about this point that I complained to him about his ferociously bad breath, which he seemed not to have noticed. I wondered what Katie made of it. He was amazed by my rudeness and pettiness and he proceeded to give me a very detailed lecture on the negative impact of rubbing ones teeth away with toothbrushes. He 'knew' that brushing caused all manner of ills before the final loss of the items in question. Bad breath was his indication of a healthy mouth and good digestive system. He certainly had active colonies of bacteria inside him. In a contest between him and a drain in summer he'd have won hands down. His breath put any self-respecting drain to shame. It was odd that I'd not really noticed his bad breath before. He probably had a digestive problem that he wasn't aware of yet. Certainly, his eating and cooking habits left much to be desired.

When we were on the last leg of our courses leading up to our final exams and consequently we were spending more time at home doing revision work. Now and then, Mick would pop around to see me and often he'd bring me a couple of cakes he'd baked or other things he'd cooked. Foolishly I ate them; often with enthusiasm because my financial state was precarious. I really should have known better though considering how well I knew his lack of hygiene. Rather stupidly, I accepted his presents of food and, even worse, I ate them. This continued for only a very short period.

Mick had invited me around for a meal and I was expecting a curry. I arrived early and saw what he was using as the main constituent. It was a plate full of sardines that had been sitting neglected on his draining board for several days. They smelt 'off'. He was only currying them to hide the bad smell. I declined Mick's invitation and went out and bought my own dinner of fish and chips. Mick was rather upset by my affront to his cooking. During his meal, he walked over to a cupboard set into one of the walls. He took out an open plastic container full of flour. I noticed that as well as flour, there were numerous little animals and droppings mixed in with it. Whilst he was in the kitchen I took a look in the cupboard and saw it was filled with all manner of packets that looked in a very sorry condition indeed. I never ate anything cooked by Mick after that—I was even reluctant to drink his coffee because he refused to accept that milk could ever be 'off'. It was always a gamble as to whether the coffee was fit for human consumption—I wasn't prepared to take that risk. Mick was never fazed and my behaviour just added to his view of me that I was squeamish.

Mick settled in quite well and was spending a lot of time practising the recorder. He had decided that the violin was not for him; he moved on to wind instead. He was madly in love with all the Beatle songs and used to try playing them on his recorder. In fact it was really a great big guessing game because he would ask me to listen and then tell him which tune he had played. I was never able to guess which tune it was because he played them with his own individual interpretation. It wasn't helped by the fact that it took him about a second to change fingers for each note. Time values meant nothing to him, neither did rhythm and timings were irrelevant. Now and then he'd con me into playing my guitar while he accompanied me. I simply strummed along but it was always shockingly horrible because I'd be waiting for him to catch me up. Our worst song was 'Let It Be'—I wish we had let it be. Mick was ever the optimist though and he persevered. I think he may have been modelling himself on Paul McCartney as far as facial hair was concerned. Paul had grown a large scruffy beard and Mick seemed to be imitating it.

I particularly remember Mick in this house because he told me some stories of things that he'd done or things that had happened to him. One of these little stories was centred on the acquisition of driving licenses. He thought they were an incredible invasion of privacy and were just another step in the state taking over—in the manner of George Orwell's Big Brother. Mick used them only because he had to but even so, he made it work his way and to his benefit, and not the way the authorities had intended. He had a whole bundle of clean licenses that he collected over a period of years. He had simply written away to say he had lost his old one and the authorities sent him a new copy. On the few occasions he'd been to court, for traffic offences, he would hand in his 'clean' license and have it endorsed. Once out of the court he simply threw the 'ruined' license away and started using another 'clean' one.

This little scheme hinged on a false address. He gave his address as that of the house where he had lived as a child. This road had been pulled down fairly recently and thus any enquiry by the police was a dead-end. The disappearance of the road meant that Mick had to rely on his supply of licenses but, I am fairly confident that he came up with another cunning scheme. Using these dodgy licenses Mick was able to elude the processes of the law without too much trouble. He almost came unstuck when he was stopped twice by the same traffic police. They remembered him from the previous time—and his scooter was still in the same unroadworthy condition. Mick was able to talk his way out of the problem but he changed his route and avoided the road where he'd been caught. It meant driving his scooter across a Common but that was no hindrance to him.

I was with him once and we were pulled to the side of the road by a large number of police who were obviously doing a traffic check. Once we had stopped we were separated and subjected to a battery of questions by plain clothed and uniformed policemen. The police didn't like the look of me. My long hair seemed to be enough to make them suspicious of me. I became sullen and unco-operative. Mick was much more streetwise; he took a completely different tack and was conversing quite openly and good-naturedly with them. Despite having no tax, insurance and the vehicle being in a terrible state they let us go. Mick had talked his way out of it with no problem whatsoever. The policemen questioning me let me go. In their eyes I was much more of a danger to society than Mick—hmmm!

There was one other occasion when we had contact with the forces of law and order. I was with him when he saw something he wanted so he stole it—it was no more than an opportunity theft. As we walked away with his ill-gotten gains we walked straight into a couple of them. With no change of pace or hesitation, Mick walked up to them and stopped them. Having got their attention, he asked them the time and then started chatting to them about what a nice day it was. We parted without any problem. He certainly could improvise. There was only one time that Mick was ever caught by the police; but that comes a bit later.

I was very surprised when Mick started a relationship with one of the local lads. He was a thug and had an air of danger about him. Most of us kept our distance but not Mick—oh no! Mr. Nasty befriended Mick and then suggested they both go for a ride on Mick's scooter; Mick thought this was a great idea. They drove northwards out of London and eventually stopped in a wood. At the suggestion of the boy they both started playing 'dare me'. This involved many things of which running naked was one of them (I remember playing this game when I was about eight or nine—remember that Mick was about thirty two at this time). After the excitement of the game, they went along to a nearby pub to get tanked up. Whilst there, they got into conversation with a group of locals.

The group consisted of two men and a woman, who was married to one of the men. They were very friendly and invited Mick and his friend back to their house. Mick and his friend went back and they were both expecting to have a pleasant sociable evening. They did. The whole lot of them ate chips and drank beer from cans until early into the morning—until they were too tired to drink anymore. Since it was so late, they were invited to stay the night by the married man. Glad not to be driving in his drunken tired state, Mick accepted the offer and was shown a spare room upstairs where he was to sleep. His friend was to sleep on the sofa downstairs. Feeling the accumulated effects of tiredness and booze Mick was soon fast asleep on the mattress and far away in the land of dreams.

His dreams were shattered by a hot breath in his ear and the feel of cold steel on his throat. The assailant was the married man. Gasping for breath Mick asked what was going on only to be told that he had to shut up or he'd have his throat cut. In silence Mick listened while his attacker explained the situation. He accused Mick of eyeing-up his wife and for trying to have sex with her. Any attempt to deny this simply moved the knife further into Mick's throat—so he thought silence was the best course. His assailant was raving mad either through too much drink, too many drugs or, more likely, too much of both. He continued accusing Mick of molesting his wife and fucking her. Despite the ridiculous charges it was no laughing matter because it was obvious that the man was intent on ending Mick's life there and then. Still holding the knife at Mick's throat, he told Mick to get up and slowly make his way to the window. Not wishing to excite the maniac, Mick complied and edged in the direction he'd been told. He soon found himself backed up to the window. Mick was told to open the window—it was a sash window and he slid the bottom section upwards. The attacker then told Mick to sit down, on the window sill, with his back facing outwards. With a knife at his throat Mick was hardly likely to disagree. The madman then told Mick to roll out of the opened window backwards. To do so would almost certainly have been fatal since it was very high up. It was the first floor and the drop was significant. It was clear that the man intended Mick to die one way or another. Stalling as long as possible, Mick tried to think of a way of escaping his tormentor whilst still keeping his life and limbs intact. It was a daunting experience.

Mick told me that suddenly everything went black and he seemed to be in the middle of a whirlwind. Somehow, Mick had freed himself from his attacker; the attacker was lying on the floor on the other side of the room. Somehow Mick had disabled his assailant; he must have pushed him away—but he had no idea how he had done it. Things were still pretty grim though and Mick had to leap out of the window (this time feet first) because his attacker was coming back, with the knife held high, for a second go.

Landing on his feet Mick made good his escape; he climbed onto the shoulder high wall bordering the garden. He raced along the wall and switched to that of an adjacent property—all the gardens were separated by similar walls. Mick escaped his tormentor. He eventually saw a light on in a kitchen and raced over to knock on the back door. Inside, a woman making a late night drink was almost shaken out of her skin. Through the door she saw Mick in all his naked glory. Through the locked door, Mick explained his situation and the woman came out of her state of shock. She left him outside and then went into her house to get some clothes for Mick to wear. She returned and passed them to him and once dressed she let him in. He told her everything about his ordeal and she listened transfixed. She suggested that he stay there for the rest of the night, which indeed he did. In the morning he thanked her and after being fed by her he said he'd go back to the house, get his own clothes, and then return the ones he'd borrowed.

Back at the madhouse he knocked on the door and it was answered almost immediately by his attacker of the night before. The attacker looked at him and with no apparent recollection of the night he asked why Mick was outside. The maniac had forgotten what he had done and Mick certainly didn't want to remind him. Mick went inside and retrieved his clothes and then went to get his friend. The friend was very surprised to hear that Mick wanted to go so soon and Mick quietly related the experiences of the night before. His friend thought this a great joke and roared with laughter. He told Mick that they were using drugs the previous night and Mick's attacker had probably been in a dream world during the attack—the attack had been very real for Mick. Mick again asked his friend to get dressed and leave with him. His friend suddenly became vicious and swore at Mick repeatedly calling him all manner of names. Mick left; he had had enough. He returned the borrowed clothes to the woman who had been so kind to him and then made his way home. His friend stayed with the loonies for a couple of weeks—he never spoke to Mick again. It was just another small chapter in Mick's life.

Our last deed inside college was to have a leaving party. The rules of non-alcohol still applied but we totally ignored this minor constraint. We invited all the assortment of strange souls to our leavers' do and most of them showed up. It was an afternoon affair. There was a superabundance of booze and most people got cheerfully drunk; a lot of dope was being consumed by the smoking brigade. I had not intended to overdo it but I surely let myself down. I was quite drunk by the time I decided to have a 'special' drink. I took a pint glass and then added a measure or two from all the bottles with anything in them. I mixed whisky, wine, beer, vodka, rum, cider and God alone knows what else. I had a brown slurry of dynamite in my glass. I downed the lot and felt incredible for a short time before passing out. I missed half the party.

I awoke mid-morning the next day lying on a sofa. The room was deserted and I was alone amid the chaotic mess of the party. The room and hallway was littered with bottles, cans, empty Party Sevens and a carpet of cigarette ends. I found it really hard to wake up and when I did I regretted it instantly. My head was exploding with a terrible headache and my stomach felt fit to do me in. In a snail-like trance I slithered to the toilet and gulped down some water. This was enough to trigger severe vomiting. I went back to my 'bed' and collapsed again. I awoke the second time in mid-afternoon as a result of the dreadful noise surrounding me. Some of my fellow party goers were tidying up. Each noise hammered into me with severe pain.

I tried to get up but couldn't move; the nausea and pain were too much. Eventually, I had no choice but to leave as the groundsmen were locking the block. I managed to crawl away from college and walk the two miles home. I was terribly ill and deserved every moment of it; I had been unbelievably stupid. I was unwell for several days; my stomach hurt because of the continual heaving but as I had not eaten anything I had nothing left to throw up. I have been drunk a few times since but never as dreadfully as that. It took several months before I could face drinking anything alcoholic again. I didn't really get to say goodbye to any of my friends as I was unavoidably detained.

College was almost over. We only had our exams to do and that was that. I had drawn up a list of revision notes with another friend of mine—Tony. Together we revised each afternoon until we knew our notes off by heart. As we completed topics we would take on board new challenges and précis them down into a revisable form. It was going really well; we were really on top of the process. I was catching up on the three years of time I had wasted. Our success was assured until Mick appeared on the scene. He asked if he could join in and we tried it once but it was impossible; he would never agree with anything we were discussing. Of course, everyone has his or her own opinions but Mick disagreed with everyone and everything and we were totally unable to work with him. It came to a crunch whilst talking about one particular educationalist. Mick had mis-read or mis-learnt something from his 'book' and kept mixing up the various ideas and the exponents responsible for them. It was impossible. In the end, I had to kick him out and we no longer allowed him to come to our sessions. Tony and I were back on track; Mick went off to do his own thing.

Our final exams took place in June and Tony and I had no real problems with passing them. As soon as the exams were over Mick came round to ask me if I'd help him move; the missionary was returning and Mick needed a new place—he needed it quickly. Using similar deceptive means as before he obtained another house to rent from an estate agent but in a different area. Once again he was told not to sublet—but of course he did. He was given a normal deal this time and he wouldn't be able to manage without someone else sharing.

Moving his stuff was much more difficult than we had thought it would be. We arrived at his place only to find that he had everything pulled out of drawers and cupboards but absolutely nothing was packed away into boxes or chests. Tony and I simply scooped up masses of his prized 'junk' and stuffed it into plastic bags and cardboard boxes from a supermarket. With the bags and boxes full we took them to the new house. This was nowhere near as nice as the one he was leaving but it was fairly good and suited his needs. It took several trips before we even started making an impression on the mountain of junk and oddments. We were both very careful not to let any of the rotting clothing near our skin for fear of rampant dermatitis etc. Tony was very good about the use of his car for the transportation; Mick didn't offer any money for petrol—why should he?

Halfway through moving his stuff we came upon a screwed up roll of five-pound notes. It would have been simple to have taken it but since both Tony and I were basically honest we took it into the next room where Mick was working. I gave it to him and he was not in the least surprised at it. He simply told us there was probably more lying about somewhere—he didn't give a damn about it.

Arriving back after a trip he told us to empty one of his cupboards. Try as we could it was impossible to get the drawers or doors open more than an inch. I went to get Mick and he said he'd nailed the doors and drawers shut to make them secure—he had made himself a safe of sorts! He walked back into the room with me and picked up an enormous poker from the fireplace and proceeded to force open the drawers and doors. The cupboard had been a rather lovely item of furniture before his intervention but it soon became so vandalized as to be beyond repair. He didn't give a damn for what the owner might think about the carnage—it didn't occur to him to have such silly thoughts.

Having cleared all his stuff we went for a final walk around the house and were amazed by the squalor that now existed. Mick had moved into a wonderfully airy, well-maintained, comfortable residence and reduced it to a shambles. The mattresses were all slashed and filthy; the tables now rested six inches off the floor and were strewn chaotically throughout the house. Several cupboard doors were hanging crookedly; why had they been vandalised? There seemed to be no good reason for the extent of the damage. It really was a mess. It seemed to mean nothing to Mick and he made no comment as he closed the door for the last time.

Mick had lost many things when the plague of hippies had been living with him. His collection of 78 records of Caruso had been taken as had the 'quiet' 45s. They had also stolen his German multi-track tape recorder; I mentioned this to him and he was not troubled at all—it was just a possession. Once again he surprised me but this time in a very positive way.

Since he hated paying rent and it would have been a struggle to meet the full cost, he sublet half the house to a recently married couple. These had both attended college with us and really should have known better than accept Mick's invitation to live with him. Actually they were rather pathetic. She was a rabid Christian and he was a watered-down 'labourite'. Between the two of them they had a very limp political outlook about how the world should be run. They allowed themselves to be totally hoodwinked by Mick despite having known him, from a distance, for a couple of years. They really thought they were on to a good thing and were unaware that they paid all the rent and more; Mick was able to live there rent free because they had it covered. When Mick told me of his deal I was very angry with him and it made our friendship become very strained again.

Our friendship ended in drama but events still needed to unroll themselves before the axe fell. I want to finish it off by describing the breakdown. Bear with me; it is a rather convoluted story but well-worth the wait. I just need to tidy up a few details first.

When Mick didn't have a scooter he had a pushbike. He had always been used to riding them—they gave him a feeling of security with which to overcome his agoraphobia. One day, he had to go to a place well outside the north of London and he looked at his outdated map and saw a road which went straight there. He got on his bike and pedalled away along the route he'd chosen. At first the journey was nothing out of the ordinary but he soon came to a very big major road. He continued along it but was soon infuriated by people in cars and lorries hooting him with their horns. It seemed as though every single vehicle that passed sounded off at him. In the end he was incensed by it all and rode along with one hand stuck up behind him. As each vehicle passed so he gave it a two-fingered salute; and not in the Winston Churchill fashion.

These toots and gestures continued for miles and miles and there seemed no way of escaping from the road. There simply weren't any side roads. The wind picked up and he soon found himself in a dangerous situation. Every time a lorry went past he felt himself sucked out into the road. It was particularly nasty when a convoy went past because as each individual vehicle went by, so he was sucked further, and further, out from the verge. At last he came to a turning off and it was only then that he realised he had cycled along a motorway. What a plonker!

Anyway, he had made it safely and stayed in the place for the day going about his business but come evening, he had to go home again. Having no lights he was a bit stuck but he didn't worry. He rode back along the same motorway—he didn't need lights because the road was fully lit-up! He ignored the hooting this time because he knew why they were doing it.

He had one other occasion of being in problems on a main road. He was on a dual carriageway and realised he had missed his turnoff. The next turnoff was not for miles and so he planned to do a U-turn across the central reservation. He got into the fast lane, which in itself was a major achievement as he was on his scooter—and suddenly pulled into the grass at the middle. Cars behind him all thought he had crashed and there was a sharp squeal of brakes but realising he was all right they carried on. In the middle of the thin strip he turned his scooter to face the other way. This was no problem but the task of getting started was. The road was thick with cars and the breaks in the traffic were minimal to say the least. Frustrated at being caught he decided to close his eyes and simply force his way out. He did. Luckily he wasn't killed. The traffic snarled to a halt as he accelerated from 0 to 30 in about thirty seconds. He was responsible for several gallons of adrenalin being released just then. I was always astonished by his stories but they were all simply matter of fact to him—just amusing little anecdotes.

CHAPTER 7

The long and winding road

Mick had been in his new place a couple of weeks when he called around to see me. He was in a dreadful state. He was shaking and eating his beard nervously and I knew something dreadful had happened. He really needed to talk to me but he was unable to control himself and couldn't speak for about half an hour. He kept muttering self-pitying comments and saying I'd despise him when I found out what he had done. This went on for a couple of hours until eventually I felt my patience run out. I told Mick he either told me his problem or shut up about it. Confronted by having to make a decision, he was forced to come to some resolution and so he chose to tell me just what the problem was. He said he was in trouble with the police. I was unmoved, as a result of being worn down for so long, I asked what he had done. He told me his story.

He told me that he had left my place the day before and was riding home on his bike. Of course he had no lights and whilst pedalling along he had suddenly come face to face with a policeman who told him to stop. He slowed down and then, when abreast of the copper, Mick lashed out with his foot and booted the bobby over.

Putting his muscles to work he tried to make his escape. Unfortunately, the policeman had dragged himself off the ground and was giving chase. There was no escape on the bicycle because it was totally useless and Mick soon found himself thrown to the ground and handcuffed. He was taken to the police station and questioned and then released while awaiting a court appearance for not having lights on a pushbike and the additional charge of assaulting a policeman. I listened to this and I half believed it but somehow I couldn't quite believe that he had hit the copper. In all the time I knew him I had never witnessed Mick hitting anyone at all. Mick had hurt lots of people but never through acts of violence. Somehow his story didn't quite hold together. I didn't mention my doubts though, since Mick seemed to have recovered his control and I didn't want him collapsing again. He left after he had finished his confession and I thought over what he told me; my doubts and uncertainties grew.

I had no time to worry about Mick, though, because I had just started working in a factory. It was dirty and gruelling and used about 99% muscle and 1% of the intelligence of the people working there. When I got home, after work, I was completely exhausted. It was a pleasing feeling though—I had worked really hard and I could feel and see my body improving from the exercise.

Mick came round again and told me that he hadn't told me the whole story about what had happened. He amended his story. The second version had a follow up piece. At the station Mick had given a false name and address and the police had no way of checking whether he was telling the truth or not. They decided to take him home at about three in the morning. They dropped him at the address he had chosen; of course they waited outside to make sure that it actually was the place where he lived. Mick knocked at the front door of the house and waited for an answer. He heard someone come grumbling downstairs and then the hall light went on as the awakened occupant opened the door. Mick simply thrust him aside and hastily closed the door behind him thus excluding the police. The man inside the house was terrified that Mick was one of these mad axe-men you read about and Mick certainly seemed a madman with his Karl Marx beard. He stayed at the house until the police car drove away and then, to the enormous relief of the householder, he left. No doubt he contacted the police immediately and thus set in motion a search for the 'madman'.

I questioned Mick and asked him if the police had any idea who he really was. He wasn't entirely sure because they had confiscated everything he had on him at the time of the arrest. Although he didn't carry any licenses or whatever he wasn't sure whether or not there was anything that could identify him. This was long before the days of credit cards and mobile phones. Mick simply didn't have any paper or plastic that could identify him. I told Mick he had probably got away with it and that he simply had to sweat it out. For several days his movements about the locality were severely constrained and he restricted himself only to travelling at night. He didn't use a bike anymore—that would have been too easy for the police to find him—he didn't have a bike anymore anyway as that had been lost when he had been arrested.

I thought I had the complete version of what had happened to Mick. Mick hadn't finished with me yet and there was more to unfold. A few evenings later Mick reappeared and said he needed to talk to me again. He told me that he had told me a pack of lies and, since I was his friend he felt bad about it and wanted me to know the truth. I felt hurt and angry. He became morose and unable to tell me what he had done. I told him to get out and come back when he was ready to talk. He said he was so ashamed and I'd think him an animal. I had no idea what he was going on about; I told him I wouldn't think anything like that but I would think him spineless if he didn't tell me what had really happened.

He suddenly calmed down and with a last nervous giggle related the true events that had led to the state of half of London's police being on his trail. He had been near the reservoir. He was on his bike and had decided to pedal back along the pathway. On his way back he met another man and stopped to talk with him. A little later they made their way into the bushes and soon were having a jolly good time. Mick stopped here and asked if I thought he was sick. I reassured him and told him to get on with it. Whilst thus engaged the two of them didn't notice a police car approaching and stop. They were caught literally with their trousers down. The other man 'scarpered' but Mick's efforts to escape brought chaos as both he and one of the policeman fell into a large muddy puddle. The other constable came to the rescue of his colleague. Mick found himself handcuffed with his arms twisted behind him—quite unnecessary of course because once he was caught he was very passive. Mick was taken off to the police station and subjected to massive abuse and called a vile pervert and so on. It really had not helped when he had caused the policeman to fall into the muddy puddle. Mick told me that he decided not to be co-operative and refused to even acknowledge their presence. After several long tiring and insufferable hours he thought out his escape and chose a phony name and address and offered to take them back there. He guessed correctly that they would let him walk into the house and leave him. This was the house he mentioned earlier.

The only thing that worried him was the fact that he couldn't be quite sure whether or not the police had any way of tracing him. Since nothing was heard for a couple of weeks we both assumed that the police had no leads and were chasing dead ends. Coincidentally, as it all dragged on, I caught a bout of summer flu. I was still working in the factory. I had continued to work, despite the flu—I was desperate to earn some money. It was a Friday, the flu had just got worse and worse—it seemed to be too bad to endure and I was convinced I would not make it through the day. Events overtook me and the flu vanished for a short time.

It was just before seven a.m. when there was a loud knocking at the front door and I went down to see who it was. As I turned the handle the door was pushed open and I found myself thrown against the wall while two violent men held me. I yelled out to my flat mates who came running. We all thought it was a gang of thugs. It was! It was the local C.I.D. They were screaming at us to let them have him. We weren't very co-operative as we had no idea what or who they were on about. They then said they wanted the man with the black beard. I knew immediately that they meant Mick. My flat mates looked at me and the police spotted this. It was obvious to all that I knew who Blackbeard was.

I was taken to one side and told to tell them where he lived. I told them I didn't know. I said we had lost contact after college had ended back in June. It sounded plausible but they weren't fully convinced. Feeling a little more confident I asked them why they thought he lived with me. I was told that he's been arrested and in his possession he had a library ticket with my name on it. They had checked the college after they lost him and after the confusion about the 'wrong' name on the ticket they quickly discovered Mick's name. A quick search of the college records had turned up my address and that's where they expected to find Mick. They asked me why he had my library ticket. I honestly had no idea—he must have 'borrowed' it from me. I didn't know that Mick had given my new address as his own either. Mick had taken a few liberties.

One of the police questioned me whilst the others started searching the flat. It became obvious that Mick really didn't live there and no one knew much about Mick except me. The questioning was getting nowhere and I told them about work and they said I could leave. They hadn't quite finished checking the flat so I left them to it. I thought that Mick had got away with it—the trail had gone cold on him. I got to work on time somehow and once in told everyone about it. As usual there was a total denouncing of the police action (the best in the world ha ha.) My flu kicked back in and I felt dreadful; I simply couldn't stand the pounding noises made by the machines. I went to the reception and told them of my complaint; I was told I could leave. I was about to go home when a message came over the intercom that I was wanted in the manager's office. This happened to be the other side of the factory and I had to walk all the way past the machines again. I entered the manager's office and, to my horror, the boot boys were there, waiting for me. One of them smirked and held up a small bag.

Inside I saw a small quantity of dope—my friends were dope heads. I was told that unless I took them to Mick they would bust us all for possession of drugs. I felt bloody awful. I had flu; I could hardly stand up from the feeling of nausea. I had to choose between busting my flat mates or busting Mick. I didn't rush to a decision despite more threats of 'and we'll get you for hindering our investigations'. Eventually I came to the conclusion that I had no choice but to shop Mick. My flat mates had done nothing wrong apart from messing around with the dope. I was presented with a choice—my friends and I could be busted for possession of drugs or I could shop Mick. I didn't make a snap decision despite the threats by the policeman. In the end I felt angry with Mick. He had stolen the library card from me. This small misdemeanour turned me against him. I told them I'd co-operate and, held by both arms, they led me out to the cars. I was pushed in to the back of one of them—just like in the films; they held my head down so that I wouldn't bang it on the top as I got in. It's funny the silly things one remembers.

They didn't say very much in the car—I was content with that and said nothing as we drove closer and closer towards Mick. I felt dreadfully nauseous and the swinging motions of the car didn't help my flu one bit.

We arrived at Mick's house and everyone got out of the cars. I was told to walk to the door in a normal fashion and then ring the bell. I was cautioned not to do 'anything silly'. I went to the door and as I did so, they took up positions from which to pounce as the door was opened. I rang the bell several times and my heart lifted temporarily; I thought

Mick was out. I thought I'd be able to sneak back a little later and warn him.

Then I heard a movement inside and singing started wafting down from upstairs. Mick came to the door and his eyes lit up when he saw me. Suddenly, I felt myself pushed aside as the strong arm of the law struck. They grabbed Mick and took him inside. One of them cautioned him and whilst doing it Mick said he was innocent and said he had no idea what was going on. One of them told him to shut up. He had been one of the officers in the station that had questioned Mick. Mick changed his moods instantly. One moment he had been shouting denials and professing innocence—the next moment I saw Mick crying and grovelling and fall to his knees. It was truly pathetic. I was dreadfully uncomfortable as I watched Mick being arrested and handcuffed in front of me.

Mick was led out and he looked at me as he passed. 'Judas—I thought you were my friend'. I was surprised by one of the policemen. He turned to Mick and told him that I had been very obstructive; they were thinking of charging me for it and also for the possession of drugs. Mick said nothing—he was in his own hell. Unfortunately, I was bitterly disappointed that he had assumed that I had 'shopped' him without a thought or a struggle. It hurt me very much; in that instant our friendship ended. The police took me home; I'd wanted to go home from work anyway. As I got out of the car one of them joined me and told me that I might still be charged for the obstruction and drugs. I listened in misery; all I could think about was my two flat mates. OK, they were dope-heads but they were gentle hippies—they wouldn't hurt a fly.

The detective spoke with me for a short time; he knew he had me over a barrel and he played his power games for a few minutes. Having made his point he and the others left. I went back into the flat and met my flat mates and told them what had happened. I had to tell them that the drug thing was still hanging over our heads and that I might be charged with obstruction. They told me that I was never to invite Mick back. I had no intention of doing that anyway. The atmosphere was chilly from then on and I knew my time at the flat was over. I stayed another month or so before moving out; my flat mates were glad to see the back of me. Nothing ever happened about the drugs—phew! What a relief.

What happened to Mick—you may well ask. It was a pathetic case of blind justice. He went to court and was fined a few pounds. The police would have done better to have 'busted' the three of us for drugs. The fines and sentences would have been much greater. On the other hand, Mick had made them look silly and they needed to sort him out—they didn't really do that though—once again, Mick escaped punishment.

Mick managed to worm his way out of trouble even at court. He asked for the process to be in camera and the magistrate agreed for some reason. So Mick's little incident never made it into the press. Just to tidy things up, he went back to college to have a word with the Principal. Any mention of scandal would have wrecked his chances of becoming a teacher. He saw her and told her that he'd been drinking and had got into a fight with the police. The Principal had no idea why the police had been after Mick—they hadn't given a reason. She asked why Mick had fought with them and he said that he'd received a letter from Australia (how conveniently distant) telling him of the death of his brother. The news had shattered him and driven him to drink. Consequently he had become involved in a drunken brawl with the police. The Principal accepted it all and even gave Mick a lecture on the evils of drink, she was a Methodist. She thanked him for giving her the 'facts' and as far as she was concerned the incident was closed. This was all Mick wanted to hear and he made good his departure from her office.

Our friendship was effectively smashed. I saw Mick once or twice afterwards but he no longer trusted me and I no longer thought him worthy of my friendship. We never said goodbye as such—we simply stopped seeing each other—we simply drifted apart. He did one more thing before he left that disappointed me. I bumped into the couple who had been sharing the house where he had been arrested. They paid him rent every week but he didn't bother to forward it to the estate agent. One day they came back and found he'd moved all his stuff out. They were in a state because they knew it was a rented property but they didn't know who to pay the rent to. They wanted to pay but couldn't. One day the estate agent called and asked for Mick. They said they were his tenants and, to cut a long story down to size, they were out on their ears in two shakes of a lambs tail (beat that for a cliché).

It's a shame that the last memories I have of him should be so disappointing but I suppose they are inevitably like that. In death, a friend ceases immediately and the good and bad points balance each other out to the extent that the good points prevail. With the demise of friendship, it is inevitable that the end is tarnished with ill feeling. No doubt he still thinks badly of me—I suppose we're both right in our own ways. Mick was such a mixture of contradictions. He was prepared to overlook the slaughter of a pig as long as he got his bacon sandwich. Despite his obsession with flowers and 'beautiful' things he was very callous. He didn't like people very much unless they were serving his purpose.

So, it all ended. The adventures with Mick were bizarre and thought provoking. Would it have been possible to remain friends with him if there hadn't been the court case—probably not? I was moving forward with my life into teaching and of necessity I had to have structure and order—I don't think Mick could have accepted the changes that took place.

The media presents the tail-end of the 1960s as a time of hippies, Flower Power and love-ins. I remember it very differently—as time spent with Mick. I am pleased that he and I shared so many adventures; I have all these stories.

POSTSCRIPT

So the question has to be—what happened to Mick? Well, I have no idea. He left the area immediately after the court case and I never heard of him or from him again. I hope that he managed to marry together his three passions of art, biology and Katie 'with the smiling eyes'. There must have been a niche somewhere for him that could have allowed him to express himself. I hope he managed to get along with people a bit better—that seemed to be his biggest problem.

I was talking with my wife very recently about Mick and me and she asked me what I thought Mick thought of me. I was stumped! I really don't know. I remained his only consistent friend over that time period except for the people who came and went very quickly. I was the one person who stood alongside him for all those years. My wife also asked me why Mick confided so much in me. He told me things about himself that he told no-one else. No-one else was party to the knowledge of his agoraphobia—this was such a cursed affliction for him. His memories about his early childhood were particularly painful—the experiences with the abusive father were horrifying.

Was Mick my role-model—my mentor? Was he a father figure? Did he impress me and mould my way into adulthood? The answer has to be no to all of these. I was young and didn't know any better—I could blame my actions on my naiveté. Mick, on the other hand, had to take full credit or blame for his own actions—he was the grown-up.

I have no memorabilia that directly links me to Mick. I know there was a single photograph of the two of us sitting on a bench on the local common. It was taken by a female art student—she was the only one who remained a friend of Mick's—and yes, he did manage to sleep with her.

It was never my intention to make Mick sound stupid or cruel. Unfortunately, many of his deeds may come across like that. I have tried to set this down as a record of what happened. Most of it happened—more or less as I have said—but four decades can play hell with one's memory. Anyway, I think I'm done now.